# The Cucumber and The Gooseberry

*by George William Johnson*

**with an introduction by Roger Chambers**

# Self Reliance Books

# *Introduction*

I am pleased to present yet another title on Currants and Gooseberries.

The work is in the Public Domain and is re-printed here in accordance with Federal Laws.

As with all reprinted books of this age that are intended to perfectly reproduce the original edition, considerable pains and effort had to be undertaken to correct fading and sometimes outright damage to existing proofs of this title. At times, this task is quite monumental, requiring an almost total "rebuilding" of some pages from digital proofs of multiple copies. Despite this, imperfections still sometimes exist in the final proof and may detract from the visual appearance of the text.

I hope you enjoy reading this book as much as I enjoyed making it available to readers again.

Roger Chambers

# CONTENTS.

## THE CUCUMBER.

# THE CUCUMBER.

## HISTORY.

THE cucumber is one of our Kitchen Garden products earliest mentioned in history. It is, and always has been, a vegetable peculiarly refreshing and agreeable to the palates of natives of warm climates; and it is among these that we first find it mentioned as a cultivated and coveted esculent. When wandering in the Wilderness more than thirty-three centuries ago (1490 B.C.), the ungrateful Israelites remembered with regret the cucumbers which they had enjoyed so abundantly when in Egypt. (*Numbers* xi. 5.) Cucumbers are still among the most extensively cultivated vegetables of that country; and I have observed entire fields of them growing on the banks of the Ganges, in Hindostan. To guard them from depredation, a watchman was here placed in a reed hut; and its isolated position most forcibly illustrated that other passage of Scripture in which this vegeta_ble is mentioned, and where the prophet foreshadows the deserted state of Zion by comparing her to "a lodge in a garden of cucumbers." (*Isaiah* i. 8.)

B

The cucumber was probably introduced into western Europe by the Romans. At all events their intercourse with Africa would render them acquainted with this vegetable; and it is quite certain that in the beginning of the first century of the Christian era they were well instructed in its cultivation. Tiberius, the emperor, was very fond of the cucumber, and by artificial means was supplied with it throughout the year. It was grown in large baskets filled with dung, covered with earth, and sheltered from the external cold by thin plates of talc, or lapis specularis, admitting the light nearly as well as modern glass. At night the baskets were removed to the shelter of some house. (*Columella lib* xi. c. 3.)

Pliny and Enthydemus confounded together the gourd and the cucumber, but Menedorus correctly distinguishes them, and calls the latter the *Indian cucumber*.

Varro says that it was called *Cucumis*, on account of the crookedness of the fruit; and the Greek name *Sicyon* was applied because its medical qualities were considered to be cooling.

The late Greek writers called it *sichysemeros*. In Dutch it is called Gurchen, from which is evidently derived our word gherkin.

The culture, as detailed by the Roman writers, *De Re Rustica*, is very coincident with our own open ground practice; and even the artifices of our gardeners are evidently descended to us from them. Thus Palladius directs that the seed shall be macerated in water before sowing, and that the fruit shall be grown in tubes to increase its length. Columella and Quintilius (A.D. 151) give similar directions, and add, among other particulars, that the fruit of the cucumber will increase in length towards water in a vase sunk in the earth a few inches from its extremity.

It is now in vain to inquire whether the Romans introduced the cucumber into England, together with the many other objects of cultivation with which they are known to have enriched our gardens ; for the first record we have of its being grown in this country is in the reign of Edward III. (1327-1377). (*Lyte's Herbal.*)

Thomas Hill, who published "The Profitable Art of Gardening," in 1563, "partly from his own experience," but certainly chiefly compiled from Varro, Cato, and Palladius, mentions "cucumbers" as products of the Kitchen Garden, but without detailing the method of cultivating them.

Conrad Heresbach, in his "Rei Rusticæ libri Quatuor," published in 1570, and translated into English by Googe, in 1578, shews that he was well acquainted with the cucumber.

In the "Gardener's Labyrinth," published by Dethicke in 1577, under the assumed name of Didimus

Mountain, there are many good directions for the culture of cucumbers. He says they are best trained upon a trellis "that the fruites corrupt not by lying on the earth;" and gives some instructions as to the mode of keeping the plants well supplied with moisture by filtering, that is, by having worsted with one end in water and the other in the soil ; says that plants raised from cuttings are soonest productive ; but all his directions are mingled with many absurdities borrowed from classic authorities.

In Lyte's " Herball," published in 1578, the cucumber is described under the botanical names it still retains (Cucumis sativus), and as the Melopepon of Galen. He does not mention any varieties, and the drawing which he gives shews that the fruit must have been very short and prickly.

Gerarde, less than twenty years after, 1597, gives the following directions for its cultivation :—A hotbed is to be made in the middle of April, or somewhat sooner, of stable-dung, an ell in breadth and depth, to be covered with hoops and poles ; (for glasses were not then known) ; and at night, mats, old painted cloth, or straw, were to be thrown over it ; the bed was to be covered with rich earth, finely sifted, half a foot thick : in this the seeds were to be sown ; and the covering being put on, was to remain seven or eight days without being taken off: the plants being then come up, were to be watered in the middle of the day with water that had stood in the house or in the sun; the covering was to be put on every night, and taken off every day; and when the plants had four or six leaves, and the danger of cold nights was past, they were to be replanted very curiously, with the earth sticking to them as near as may be, unto the most fruitful place, and where the sun had most force in the garden; covering them with dock-leaves or wisps of straw, propping up with forked sticks, to keep them from the cold of the night and the heat of the sun. (*Gerarde's Herball,* 764.)

Gerarde mentions *Cucumis vulgaris,* the cowcumber or cucumber, which is our short prickly cucumber, and *Cucumis ex Hispanico,* or Spanish cucumber. These are the only two kinds he describes; for his *C. Turcicus, C. anguina,* and *C. pyriformis,* are mere gourds. His Spanish cucumber appears to be the first improved variety of which we have any notice. Gerard says of it, " There hath been, not long since, sent to Strasburgh, in Germany, out of Spain, some seeds of a rare and beautiful cucumber; the fruit of a foot in length." He then gives directions for making a hotbed, which have been detailed: all which directions, he says, if followed, would enable the gardener to defy " the intemperancy of the climate although in the farthest parts of the north of Scotland." Gerard says that the cucumber, if eaten breakfast, dinner, and supper, for three weeks without intermission, it "doth perfectly cure all manner of sauce-phlegm and copper faces, red and shining fiery noses (as red as red roses), with pimples, pumples, rubies, and such like precious faces!"

In a few years subsequently glass began to be employed for the protection of the plants, though the ignorance under which gardeners laboured, as to the mode of forcing, was still extreme. Thus, Parkinson, in his "Paradisus," published in 1627, although he directs the cucumber to be sown in a hotbed, it was not to be done until April, and the plants were to be removed to a rich soil, without bottom heat, and to be "covered with straw (some do use great hollow glasses, like unto bell heads) or some such other things, to defend them from cold and the heat of the sun, while young and new planted." Of "cowcumbers" he enumerates six varieties, viz.:—1. The long green, much ribbed. 2. The short, of equal size throughout. 3. Long yellow, yellowish, 13 inches long, but "not the cucumis anguinis of the Latins." 4. The French. 5. Dantzic, small, and imported in a pickled state. 6. Muscovy, smallest of all, "no bigger than small lemons."

From bell glasses the transition to frames, and other more regular forcing structures, was easy and rapid, so that Switzer, writing in 1727, boasts, that cucumbers, which twenty-five years before were never seen at table until the close of May, were then always ready early in March, or even sooner if tried for. Mr. Fowler, gardener to Sir Nathaniel Gould, at Stoke Newington, was the most successful cultivator of the cucumber, and the first to raise plants in autumn for fruiting about Christmas; and he presented the king, George the 1st, with a brace of full-grown cucumbers, on the New Year's Day of 1721. (*Bradley's General Treatise on Husbandry*, ii. 61.)

The first separate treatise on the growth of the cucumber, with which I am acquainted, was published in 1717, by Samuel Collins, Esq., of Archester, in Northamptonshire, and is, in his work, entitled, "Paradise Retrieved." He then knew only three varieties, "the long smooth, the short prickly, and a particular kind, 15 inches long, scarce amongst us." His directions for their culture, under hand glasses and frames, are very full and correct.

Switzer alludes to there being, formerly, only three varieties of the cucumber, but adds, that in his time there were eight, and, with few exceptions, his directions for their culture in hotbeds is nearly as full and satisfactory as that now given by authorities a century later. Of course, improvements in the structure of the frames, and other appliances, have since been made, but his practice was, for the most part, very correct, and as his immediate successors were Fairchild and Miller, I have no need to trace the progress of its culture further. Our present practice is only a modification of theirs.

Cucumbers are now very extensively cultivated for the public markets. In Hertfordshire and Bedfordshire many acres are annually devoted to their growth—the fruit to be gathered small for pickling—and the amount may be estimated from the fact stated by Mr. Loudon, that the village of Sandby, in the county last named, has been known, in one week, to furnish 10,000 bushels of gherkins.

---

## BOTANICAL CHARACTERS.

THE cucumber *(Cucumis sativus)* is one of the species belonging to the Monoecia Monadelphia class and order of Linnæus, and of Cucurbitaceæ in the Natural System. It is a trailing annual.

*Root*, annual: *stems*, creeping, hispid, rough: *leaves*, heart-shaped, with sharp, projecting, terminating angles: *flowers*, yellow, axillary; germ oblong, obscurely angular, not hairy, but muricatad with prickles springing from a smooth warty substance: *fruit*, elongated, almost cylindrical, obtuse at both ends; scabrous, with warts, yellowish, white, or green, in different varieties; rind thin, coriaceous; flesh spongy; primary cells three or four, each divided into two secondary cells, and then again into the proper cells of the seed, filled with a pellucid jelly. Supposed to be a native of Tartary.

Upon the physiology of the cucumber I have only to observe, that in several instances I have noticed a remarkable difference in the number of tendrils produced by plants of the same variety, the long prickly, according to the situation in which they were grown. Those plants, the stems of which were allowed to trail along the surface of the soil, produced very few tendrils, and these in no one instance reached to any length. Other plants, from the same sowing, trained upon an inclined plain of hazel boughs, produced many more tendrils, and these grew to a far greater length and were of much service to the plants, in enabling them to cling to their more elevated position. This is only one of many instances of a wise provision and adaptation of the organs to circumstances. M. de Candolle thought, that the tendrils of the cucumber would have been stipules if circumstances required, but some observations of Dr. Bell Salter lead to the conclusion, that they would be leaves if the plants required a larger surface of foliage.

## CHEMICAL COMPOSITION.

THE fruit of the cucumber has been analyzed by Dr.

John, who found it composed of the following ingredients :—

| | |
|---|---|
| Water .. .. .. | 97,13 |
| Substance similar to fungin .. | 0,53 |
| Soluble vegetable albumen .. | 0,13 |
| Resin .. .. .. | 0,04 |
| Extractive with sugar .. | 1,66 |
| Mucus .. .. | |
| Phosphate of lime.. | |
| Phosphate of potash | |
| Phosphoric acid .. | |
| Ammoniacal salt .. | 0,5 |
| A malate .. | |
| Sulphate of potash | |
| Muriate of potash.. | |
| Phosphate of iron.. | |

(*Journ. de Physique*, xxix. 3.)

The fact of the cucumber containing a substance analogous to fungin, the constituent which imparts a poisonous quality to some of the mushroom tribe, is a sufficient explanation of the fact that this vegetable is so offensive to the stomachs of some persons.

---

## VARIETIES.

THESE are numerous, and from time to time others are announced; but let it not always be taken for granted that these are new or meritorious.

### FOR OPEN-GROUND CULTIVATION

The following are well suited :—

*Early short Prickly.* Four inches long, green,

smooth, prickles black and few. Very hardy, and, when an early abundant crop is more considered than length or beauty of proportion, it may be selected as the best for winter forcing. Sometimes called the *Old Southgate.*

*Early long Prickly.* Best for summer crop. About six inches long, otherwise resembles the first-named. Both are good bearers.

*Longest green Prickly.* Differs from the preceding in being about nine inches long, and not an early bearer. The prickles are black, and very numerous.

*Early green Cluster.* Has its blossoms three or four together. Very early; five inches long; has many tendrils, which renders it easily trainable upon sticks or other treillage. Leaves small, and growth compact. The *Gherkin* is a name sometimes given this variety.

*White Dutch Prickly.* Early, and of peculiar agreeable flavour. Seeds few.

## FOR FORCING UNDER FRAMES.

*White Turkey, Green Turkey.* These have straight smooth fruit, about 16 inches long. They have robust, large leaves, and are shy, very late bearers.

*Green Roman.* This, like the two preceding, has fruit destitute of prickles, and about the same length. It is a robust grower, but earlier than the Turkey.

*Flanagan's.* Length of fruit two feet; very green; black prickles; crisp and good.

*Nepaul.* Has a very large fruit, 17 inches long and 8 inches in diameter. A native of Nepaul, unsightly for table, but good for stewing.

*Duncan's Victoria.* A seedling, named in honour of her Majesty; is one of the finest. Colour, deep green. Set with spines to the shoulder, thick and black. Shoulder short. Fruit uniform and straight, growing to a great length. Mr. Duncan has had them 28 inches long; 24 inches in nine days from setting; and sometimes 4 inches long previously to the expansion of the bloom. It is a great bearer, but does not force so well as shorter kinds.

*New Roman Emperor.* Fruit, beautiful and excellent; forces well. Length, 24 inches. White-spined, but closely set with them to the shoulder. Colour, deep green, and fruit uniform throughout. Capital bearer, quick grower, and well adapted for general culture.

*Allen's Victory of Suffolk.* Fruit, beautiful, when grown in a good heat, and cut in an early age. Uncommonly slender, exceedingly tender, and does not force well. It seldom grows longer than 20 or 24 inches. Spine black, and thickly set; and is the handsomest fruit grown.

*Sion House.* Famous for winter culture, and in pots. Colour, shining green; almost devoid of spines; never growing longer than 8 or 9 inches. Great bearer, hardy, and altogether one of the best of the winter cucumbers.

*Cure's Stove Cucumber.* Solely suited for winter culture, either in the stove or in frames. Length, 9 or 10 inches. Black spine, and a good-looking fruit. A capital bearer, and early habit.

*Hort's Early Frame.* Very early, growing to the length of 8 or 10 inches. Spine black, and colour deep green. Well adapted for winter forcing, and as early as any other. Fruit may be cut in eight weeks, in winter, from the sowing of the seed.

*Stradsett Park.* A fruit of surpassing excellence. Length, 26 or 27 inches. Slender. Somewhat resembling Allen's Victory, but surpasses it. Colour, pale green; spine, black, and thickly set. It was raised by Mr. D. Stewart, of Stradsett.

*Stewart's Nonpareil.* A fruit intermediate between Stradsett Park and Allen's Victory, One of the best in cultivation, but not so deep colour as some are. Spine, black. Slender. Length, 26 or 27 inches. It does not force well, and requires a strong constant heat to bring it to perfection. It was raised by Mr. Stewart, and obtained first prizes in 1839.

*New Sion House.* Similar to the preceding of the same name, and corresponds with it, except in length and hardy habit; forces well, and is a good bearer.

Length, two feet and upwards, beautiful, slender, and uniform.

*Weedon's Cucumber* was raised by the author of a very excellent little treatise on the cucumber. It is a handsome black spined, good fruit, forces well, and is a good bearer. Length, fifteen or sixteen inches. A variety of this, called *Weedon's Improved,* has gained the first prize at Ipswich.

*Warham Champion* has black spines, deep green colour, short shoulder, and attains in some cases a length of 20 or 24 inches. It is a good, beautiful, slender-growing kind, and succeeds well trained against a south wall, or on ridges.

*Barne's Man of Kent* is said to force pretty well, and to attain to a length of 20 or 24 inches. Colour, deep green ; spine, black.

*Manchester Prize Fighter* is of acknowledged excellence, raised in the neighbourhood of Manchester. It was second on the list for prizes at the Heaton Norris Cucumber Show, in 1840. It is a great bearer, has white spines, is slender in its proportions, and grows to the length of 24 inches. It is sometimes called *Walker's Prize Fighter.*

*Walker's Pea Green* was first on the list at the above show, in 1840. (*Duncan's Cucumber Culture,* 89.)

*Young's Champion.* Fruit two feet long, green,

white spined, excellent for winter forcing, being hardy and prolific.

*Kenyon.* A moderate sized kind, very generally prefered for early forcing near Liverpool.

*Superb White Spine.* Fruit about 22 inches long; shape handsome, hardy, and a good bearer.

*Latter's Victory of England.* Black spined, hardy, and long, but very deeply ribbed. A great favourite at Ipswich.

*Brownston Hybrid.* Long, handsome, black spined. Like the last, it has gained many prizes, but neither are very prolific, and require a high temperature.

*Cuthill's Black Spine.* Very prolific, length of fruit about 16 inches, good for early forcing.

The *Snake* is very slender, and attains the length, it is said, of 12 feet; and the *Fluted*, from China, has remarkably indented fruit, but these have no particular merits. *Ringleader, Tiley's Victory of Bath,* and *Pratt's Hybrid,* are good varieties, and have gained many prizes.

---

## STANDARD OF MERIT.

DR. LINDLEY, after noticing that in all prize rules the superiority of the fruit is made to depend upon its length, combined with certain other qualities, justly observes, that though some of these qualities

are of importance, others are of little or no consequence ; and one, requiring the cucumber to be
ribbed, is most absurd. Why a ribbed cucumber
should be prefered to one with an even surface, seems
difficult to divine. In peeling, the portion of it beneath the rind must necessarily be cut away ; and,
consequently, great waste, as well as loss of the best
part of the fruit, is occasioned. It is equally incom-
prehensible, why a black spined cucumber should be
peremptorily declared to be superior to one with
white spines.

Qualities such as these are perfectly arbitrary,
add nothing to the appearance of a cucumber on the
dinner-table, and have no relation to its good quality
as a salad.

Then, cucumbers must be grown to an enormous
length ; everybody wants to have his fruit longer
than his neighbour's ; and if it is so long that no dish
can be found to hold it, so much the better. But is
there any common sense in this? Of what use are
these long fruits, except to make people stare? Are
they better flavoured ?—better bearers ?—better
seeders? Quite the contrary : they are simply
longer, indeed too long to be placed on a dinner-
table, too long to be eaten by a small party, too
coarse to suit a cultivated palate, and are, in fact, fit
for nothing, except to excite the admiration of the
servants' hall.

If such things must be had to stare at, why not cultivate the Patagonian Cucumber, or the Snake Gourd, at once? The fact is, that a cucumber, 10 or 12 inches long, is much better in all respects, only it is not so extraordinary, and will not cause so much amazement.

Let a cucumber, adds Dr. Lindley, be a foot long, straight, of even thickness, with a flower still fresh upon its point; let it, moreover, be short necked, firm, brittle, and a free bearer, and you have nearly all that it is possible to desire. If, of the old prickly race, bloom—natural, not artificial—should be insisted on, because it ensures carefulness on the part of the grower, and the fruit looks better; but as cucumbers of the Smyrna and Turkish breed have no bloom, and they are among the best for the table, to require bloom as a *sine qua non*, is to exclude some of the most useful sorts in cultivation.

Finally, no cucumber show should be held later than June. In proportion, as the season advances, does the difficulty of growing this vegetable diminish; and it must be some very extraordinary circumstance indeed, that can render any cucumber worth a prize after June, in a society especially instituted for its cultivation. (*Gard. Chron.*, 1843. 19.)

It is observed above, that the bloom on the cucumber should be natural, not artificial, and very wisely, for as Mr. Fulton, gardener to Lord Northwick, observed, the art of producing and keeping a fine natural bloom on cucumbers, either for a gentleman's table, for show, or for the market, merits great attention, both as to the perfect appearance of the fruit, and requires especial care to the general culture of the plant after the fruit is set. From that time a strong bottom heat should be given, and water plentifully, always at the back part of the frame; and at no time over their leaves, if the fruit is wanted for its delicate bloom and long regular shape. A fine foliage over all the bed is also a very essential point; and leaves should never be picked off near the fruit. Air, also, should be given very sparingly in the middle of the day, even in bright sunshine, and generally there should be a little admitted in the night, when the bottom heat is very strong, as by that means the air in the frames is kept sweet.

When the fruit has to travel, great care should be taken to pack it in narrow wooden boxes, in the largest stinging-nettle leaves that can be got, filling up the interstices with well-thrashed moss, and covering over with soft leaves of any kind. (*Gard. Mag.*, vi. 709.)

Relative to the rule in favour of black-spined cucumbers, it can only be because the best of the long varieties so characterized are more difficult to raise than the best of the white-spined, the latter usually not requiring so high a temperature.

Consonant with these considerations the following are given as absolute requisites in the standard of merit :—Length, not less than 12 inches ; diameter, one-ninth of the length ; colour, dark green ; spines, numerous, and equally distributed ; bloom, unremoved ; circumference, circular and equal throughout ; neck and nose, each not more than a diameter long ; flesh, crisp and juicy ; flower, remaining on the fruit. In conformity with these, the annexed is a convenient tabular form in which the judges may award the prizes.

| Prize | 1st | 2nd |
|---|---|---|
| Exhibitor | Richard Good | |
| Sort | Sion House | |
| Mode of culture | Hot-water pit | |
| Length | 18 inches | |
| Diameter | 2 inches | |
| Form | Circular&equal throughout | |
| Colour | Deep green | |
| Neck | 2 inches | |
| Nose | $1\frac{1}{2}$ inch | |
| Spine | Numerous and regular | |
| Bloom | Perfect | |
| Flesh | Crisp and juicy | |
| Blossom | Remaining | |
| General aspect | Very handsome and vigorous | |

E. CUTHILL,
T. WILD, } Judges.

## SOIL.

A FRESH loam, rather inclining to lightness than tenacity, as the top spit of a pasture, with the turf chopped fine and mixed, is, perhaps, as good a soil as can be employed for the cucumber. It will succeed in any rich open soil of the garden, for the handglass and natural ground crops. Some gardeners, however, for the forced plants, prefer a compost; and the one most generally approved is one third top spit earth, from a rich upland pasture, one third vegetable mould, one sixth well decomposed loose dung, and one sixth drift or sea sand.

That the cucumber will thrive productively in a soil abounding in decomposing organic matters is evident from the following statement by Mr. Whitmore, gardener at Falkborne Hall, Essex:

" The soil I use for all my cucumbers is nothing but decayed sawdust, and in which they seem to luxuriate. Observing a large heap of soil in the wood yard, which had for some years been carried from the saw pit, I had some of it carted to the melon ground; I then formed my hills entirely of it, and when it was warm, turned into it my plants. In a few days the hills were one mass of roots; I then, by degrees, earthed my bed with the same. The plants made shoots as thick as the finger, and by judicious stopping and thinning, bore abundantly. Many good

gardeners who saw them said, that if they had not
had ocular demonstration of the fact they could not
have believed it possible for cucumbers to flourish in
rotten sawdust.

" My plants in the pinery are in seakale pots, in
the same material; their fruit and foliage have been
the admiration of everybody who has seen them;
some of the leaves measured 22 inches across, and
are of a dark green colour, approaching to black."
(*Gard. Chron.*, 1846. 405.)

Mr. Mills, gardener to Baroness de Rothschild,
and one of our most successful cucumber cultivators,
says, that for it, peat, alone, is the best soil. He
prefers that which lies upon a subsoil of gravel, and
not more than 4 inches thick, and only requires to be
chopped up and used immediately, without addition
or keeping. (*Mills, on the Cucumber*, 15.)

Mr. Duncan, another judicious cultivator of this
plant, and gardener to T. Daniel, Esq., Henbury-
near Bristol, gives the following good practical direc
tions regarding the soil :—

" The soil should never be trod, or rendered compact; neither should heavy or clayey soil be used,
though, of course, a heavier kind is necessary in the
summer than in the winter. Vegetables, whose nature is to produce fruit in succession, like the cucumber, receive the greater amount of nourishment in the
period immediately preceding the perfecting of their

fruit; hence it is a practice with me to supply a new store of soil, at intervals, during their growth, and always previously to a time of more than ordinary interest, such as horticultural exhibitions. This soil is supplied as a casing over the whole surface when the plants are trained upon trellises, as most of ours are, but when extending over the soil the branches are laid successively, in a proportion of new mould, which is the same thing; hence, I always provide a shallow depth at first, that I may have an opportunity of affording a new supply when it is most needed.

"To render the pasture soil fit for use, it should be frequently turned and exposed to the action of the weather; and in the winter, previous to using, a fourth of cow dung, or vegetable mould, added to it; or, in the absence of these, leaf mould and frame dung. Pigeon's and sheep's dung are more stringent, in consequence of the saline matter they contain, and are very appropriate for adding, as a casing, both for plants in the soil and in the pots, or when it is intended or desired to have fruit of extraordinary fineness, and plants of vigorous growth.

"Neither the soil of the bed, nor on the linings, should be deeper than 10 or 12 inches, including those additions of soil made in the latter periods of culture. A less depth will not be sufficient, particularly if the plants are of a vigorous growth.

"The inclination of the soil in the bed, throughout the process, should be such as to facilitate the absorption of the solar rays. Cucumber soil should never be sifted; all that is necessary may be effected by turning and exposure, and a little careful disintegration. This will preserve the best parts, and prevent any from being rejected. I never allow the soil I intend using in the following year to be exposed to excess of rain; and it is a good plan in respect to this, in frosty weather, to remove the frozen part every day into an open shed. It will become by this means, when it is required for use, in fine condition, and the eggs of insects, &c., and the common earth worm, will be destroyed." (*Duncan's Cucumber Culture*, 33.)

## MANURES.

If the crop be grown in the soil of the bed, and not in pots, that soil being of the fertile composition I have directed, no other fertilizer will be required by the plants. If grown in pots, or other confined portions of earth, then *liquid manure* may be given to them with advantage. This may be made according to Mr. Ayre's formula, given under the head "STOVE CULTURE," or it may be prepared from guano, half an ounce being mixed thoroughly with each gallon of water.

A solution of *nitrate of soda,* one ounce to a gallon of water, and applied once a fortnight, is said to increase the vigour of the plants. The same is said of *common salt,* and that it does not even injure their leaves if poured over them. A very weak solution of *muriate of ammonia,* not more than half an ounce to two gallons of water, has been applied beneficially, to invigorate weak plants. I state these facts without recommending the adoption of the practice, because I know that the chief of our most successful cucumber growers do not employ any saline manures.

----

## MODES OF PROPAGATION.

*By Seeds.*—Plants raised from seeds are the most vigorous, and produce the largest fruit, therefore they should always be raised in this mode when this is to be exhibited. Indeed, it is the best to employ during the months from November to March, both inclusive. Mr. Duncan says, the best time for raising plants, by either seed or cuttings, for winter culture, is in the first and last weeks of September.

If the production of fine fruit is the object, and the sowing is any time from autumn to early spring, do not remove the seed from the parent cucumber until it is actually required for insertion in the soil; but if an abundant crop, rather than fine specimens, then seed which is one, two, or more years old, may be advantageously employed. To test the quality of the seeds they should be put into a vessel of water, and only those be sown which sink. The seeds which float are unfertile.

Cucumber seeds will retain their germinating power for eight or ten years.

*Propagation by Cuttings.*—Cuttings five or six inches in length, taken from the tops of bearing branches of vigorous plants, from about the end of March to the close of October, planted in pots of rich mould and plunged in a hotbed, or bark bed in a stove, where the temperature is not less than 70 degrees, will take root, if regularly watered, in less than a fortnight, and may then be planted in a hot-bed for fruiting, which they will do as soon as the roots can support them, perfecting the fruit before Christmas. They may thus be had in succession, and being propagated from year to year, are rendered, as if it were, perennial. The plants are less succulent, and, consequently, less liable to damp off, or suffer from the low temperature to which they are liable to be exposed in severe seasons. Mr. Mearns puts four inches and a half of mould in pots nine inches deep, in which the cuttings are planted and watered, the tops of the pots being covered with flat pieces of glass, which answer the purpose of a hand light, whilst the sides of the pot afford a sufficient shade until the roots are formed.

When the plants have afforded their first crop, any small fruit must not be waited for, but the plants be cut back to the lowest shoot, the soil gently stirred and a little fresh spread over the surface; the same attention must be paid them as before, when they will shoot afresh and produce a good crop. (*Johnson's Mod. Gard. Dict.*, 180.)

Propagation by cuttings is truly said not to be a system deserving adoption, except, when of any variety there is a short supply of seed, and it is desired to increase the stock of a new variety. Great attention is required for the first two months in stopping and thinning the fruit, cuttings being much more prolific than plants raised from seed, showing much more fruit than the plants are able to bring to maturity, so that without stopping and thinning they will very soon be exhausted. (*Gard. and Flor.*, iii. 102.)

*Layers.*—If a branch of a cucumber vine be pegged down beneath the soil, so that a joint be buried an inch or more beneath its surface, roots will be thence emitted, and the extremity of the branch will become a separate plant. This is not so easy a mode of increasing the numbers of a particular plant as by cuttings, added to which, if many of the branches are layered, though these become plants, the parent stem frequently is rendered weak, and even dies altogether.

Another mode of layering is as follows :—" Suspend, in convenient places, pots having large holes beneath; through these holes the points of growing shoots are introduced, and the pots having a little moss in the bottom, are then lightly filled with vegetable mould: they may also be propagated by enveloping a joint of a growing shoot lightly with moss; the moss should be kept continually moist, and roots will soon be emitted into it, and when enough are produced, the plant may be detached." (*Moore's Cultivation of the Cucumber*, 26.)

## OPEN-GROUND CULTURE.

The sowing for these crops must be performed at the close of May, or early in June. A rich south-west border, beneath a reed or other fence, is peculiarly favourable, as the plants then enjoy a genial warmth without suffering from the meridian sun. The border being dug regularly over, and saucer-like hollows, about fifteen inches in diameter and one or two deep, formed five feet apart, the seed may be sown six or eight in each.

Seed may also be sown beneath a hedge of similar aspect, and the plants either trained to it or to bushy branches slightly sloping from the perpendicular. If the weather be dry, it is requisite to water the patches moderately, two or three days after sowing. In four or five, if the season is genial, the plants will make their appearance, and until they have attained their rough leaves, should be guarded from small birds, which will often destroy the whole crop by devouring the seminal leaves.

If the season be cold and unfavourable, plants may be raised in pots under a frame or hand-glasses, as directed for those crops; to be thence transplanted, when of about a month's growth, or when the third rough leaf appears, into the open ground, shelter being afforded them during the night. Water must be given every two or three days, in proportion to the dryness of the season, applying it of an afternoon, or early in the morning.

Allow no more than two, or at most three, plants to grow together in a patch, about nine inches apart from each other. Attend to the training as for the frame crops; but stopping is seldom needed, the plants rarely being over-luxuriant. They will have fruit ready for use in August and September. (*John-son's Dict. Mod. Gard.* 181.) See General Culture.

Mr. Ayres says that a considerable portion of heat may be worked by artificial means into the soil for the open-ground crop. Thus, when the bed has been the marked out, let the soil be dug over in the evening of every sunny day, and then either raked perfectly smooth or covered with mats or litter; in this way the radiation of accumulated heat being nightly intercepted, a sufficient quantity of heat will in a week or ten days be collected to raise the temperature 8 or 10 degrees above that of the adjoining soil. Those who have no garden ground, but have yards or balconies on a south, east, or west exposure, may plant them in very rich compost, in large pots, or boxes eighteen inches or two feet square, and train the plants to the wall. They will require precisely the same treatment in watering, stopping, &c. as directed for pots in the cucumber-house. (*Ayres's Treatise on the Cucumber*, p. 41.)

## CULTURE UNDER HAND GLASSES.

THE first sowings for these crops must be in the last two weeks of March; to be repeated in the middle of April and May. The seed may be inserted in a moderate hotbed under hand-glasses, or in the upper side of one of the frames already in production, either in pots as directed for the frame crops, or in the earth of the bed, to be pricked into a similar situation when of four or five days' growth, inserting only two plants, however, in each pot. They must remain in the hotbed until of about a month's growth, or until they have attained four rough leaves; being then stopped they are fit for ridging out finally.

The ridges may be founded on the surface, or in trenches a foot and a half deep, in either case forming them of well prepared hot dung, three or four feet wide and two and a half high; the length being governed by the number of hand-glasses, between each of which three feet and a half must be allowed.

The earth is to be laid on eight inches thick ; when this becomes warm the plants may be inserted two, or at most three, under each glass.

It is an excellent plan to slope the surface of the soil and cover it with straw on reeds laid straight and thatchlike to shoot off excessive rains, to keep the fruit clean, and to preserve moisture to the roots in dry weather. The same treatment applies to the open ground crop.

Watering, airing, covering. &c., must be conducted with the precautions directed to be practised for the frame crops. The glasses should be kept on as long as possible without detriment to the plants; to prolong the time, the runners must be made to grow perpendicularly ; and still further to protract their continuance, if the season is inclement, the glasses may be raised on bricks. When no longer capable of confinement, the runners must be pegged down regularly, advantage being taken of a cool cloudy day to perform it in ; but the glasses, even now, may be continued over the centre of the plants until the close of May or early in June, with considerable advantage. Weeds must be carefully removed. Waterings should be performed as often as appears necessary.

If there be a scarcity of dung, in the last week of April, or during May, circular holes may be dug, two feet in diameter, one deep, and four apart. These being filled with hot dung, trod in moderately firm, and earthed over about eight inches, are ready for either seeds or plants. With the shelter of the hand-glasses they will be scarcely later in production than the regular ridges. (*Johnson's Dict. Mod. Gard.* 180.)

## HOTBED CULTURE.

*Forcing Ground.* The aspect and declination of this is of very great importance; not so much on account of the atmospheric warmth which may be thus secured, though this is available and beneficial, as on account of the utmost amount of light being desirable. Food and heat are of benefit to the plants only in proportion to the light enabling the leaves to elaborate the sap which those other contingencies enable the roots to imbibe.

Upon this point we have these practical remarks from Mr. Duncan:

" Those gardens lying open to the sun, especially in the morning, having an angle of 8 or 10 degrees S. or S.W. or S.E., are much earlier than those not so steep, or not so well exposed. No winter forcing will succeed well that is not under the congenial influence of the solar rays. A slight declination, especially on a porous subsoil, will permit the absorption of all those rays that pass over on a contrary inclination; but in summer it is of less consequence, because the rays are more perpendicular, and strike everywhere, should there be no obstacle to prevent them. If local considerations permit, the figure of the ground should be a parallelogram, having a roadway dividing it longitudinally into two unequal parts, the larger being the north side. The pits should be placed on the division south of the road, allowing a border from the boundary wall of 10 or 12 feet. There should be room enough between the pits and border for linings and a walk, without interfering with the pits on one side, or the border on the other. The dung beds should be placed in a line parallel with the pits, on the other side of the road, and far enough from it for the linings of the beds; other arrangements are necessary for soil, dung, leaves, &c. and at one side there should be a shed or sheds for keeping the frames and lights in, and for potting, and to keep pots, soil, &c. The whole space within the line of business shonld be paved, sloping towards the south, to keep the ground clean and dry, and to collect the water escaping from the beds. (*Duncan's Culture of Cucumber*, 120.)

The forcing ground must be so situated as to be entirely free from the overshadowing of trees, buildings, &c. A reed fence surrounding it on all sides is a shelter that prevents any reverberation of the wind, an evil which is caused by paling or other solid inclosure. This must be ten feet high to the northward or back part, of a similar height at the side, but in front only six. The wicket or gate must be of sufficient width to admit a loaded wheelbarrow. An inclosure of this description, 100 feet in length and 60 broad, will be of a size sufficiently large for the pursuit of every description of hotbed forcing. But for cucumbers, melons, and a few inferior articles, a space for six or eight lights is sufficient. Fruit may be forced slightly by being trained within it on the southern aspect; the fence on that side in that case must be of brick or wood. To prevent unnecessary labour this inclosure should be formed as near to the stable as possible.

For the reception of the bed, a trench is often dug of its determined length and breadth, and six inches deep, if the soil is wet, or 18 inches or more if it is dry. In a dry soil or climate this cannot be productive of much injury, but otherwise it almost always chills the bed ; at the same time it is to be observed that it is never productive of benefit, further than, not being so high, it is easier of access, but gives much additional trouble, both at the time of founding and afterwards, when linings are to be applied.

*Time and Mode of Sowing.* Sow for the earliest crops in the last week of September, also in October, November, and December, and two or three times a month during January and following months, until the middle of May. All these sowings should be plentiful, especially the earliest ones, as failures are in these sowings most likely to occur. If fruit be required for Christmas, the sowing should be the first week in August; for it is quite certain that it is easier to provide fruit then, or at any other given time, by getting the plants into bearing about a month previously, than by attempting to have the first fruit at the time desired.

*Seedling Bed.* This need be no larger than is sufficient to be covered by a one or two-light frame. Mr. Mills says that it should be three feet high at the back and two feet six inches in front; and when the lights are put on, eight or ten days should be allowed for the bed to sweeten before the seeds are sown; during which time the surface of the bed should be forked over every other day, about a foot deep; and, should it appear dry, as much water should be given as will make it moderately wet. Air must be admitted by raising the lights at the back with a wooden wedge, according to the quantity found necessary to be given to allow the steam to pass off freely. In order to prove whether or not the bed be sweet, shut the lights down close for three or four hours; then take a lighted candle in a lantern, push down one of the lights, and put the candle and lantern into the frame; and if the candle continues to burn, the bed will be in a fit state to receive the plants or seeds. (*Mills' Treatise on Cucumber*, 13.)

The soil of the Seedling Bed need not be more than five or six inches deep. The seeds are best sown four together in small pots, and plunged in the earth of the bed; the seed not buried more than half an inch deep. When the seminal leaves are half an inch in breadth, those in the earth of the bed must be pricked three together in small pots, quite down to their leaves in the earth, which should be brought to the temperature of the bed before this removal, by being set in it for a day or two previously; those seedlings that have been raised in pots must likewise be thinned to three in each. They must remain plunged in the hotbed until their rough leaves have acquired a breadth of two or three inches, when they are fit for ridging out finally.

During this first stage of growth, great care must be taken that air is admitted every day as freely as contingent circumstances will admit, as also at night, if the degree of heat and steam threatens to be too powerful. It must never be neglected to cover the glasses at night, apportioning the covering to the temperature of the air and bed. The heat should not exceed 80 deg. in the hottest day, or sink below 65 deg. during the coldest night. If the heat declines, coatings of hot dung are to be applied in succession to the back, front, and sides, if that source of heat be employed. As the soil appears dry, moderate waterings must be given, care being taken not to wet the leaves. The best time for applying it is between ten and two of a mild day, the glasses being closed for an hour or two after. The temperature of the water must be between 65 deg. and 80 deg. The interior of the glass should be frequently wiped to prevent the condensed steam dropping upon the plants, which is very injurious to them. If the bed attains a sudden violent heat, the necessary precautions to prevent the roots of the plants being injured or scalded must be adopted; but if hot water is the source of heat, this danger is avoided altogether. (*Johnson's Dict. Mod. Gard.* 176.)

Raising cucumber plants in the early part of the season causes much anxiety to gardeners having limited conveniences at their command, and especially where they have nothing to depend upon but fermenting material, for not only have they five or six week's trouble in preparing dung to form a seed-bed, but after that is formed, they have three weeks or a month to wait before the plants are fit to ridge out on the fruiting-beds.

This, to a small grower, is not only a great trouble, but a serious expense; therefore, a system of packing that will ensure the safe transmission of cucumber plants to a distance of a hundred miles or more, at the time the thermometer registers several degrees of frost, will not be without use to some. The materials necessary to secure this are two boxes, one of a size suitable to hold the plants, and the other about four inches larger every way; a quantity of dry moss, some carded wool, and a thick woollen cloth, similar to those used for horses. In packing the plants, which should be hardened for three or four days previously, by being placed in a moderately dry heat of from 55 to 60 degrees, a little moss must be put on the surface of each pot, and secured down with matting.

A small stake should be placed in the centre of each pot, and the plants should be secured to it, so as to make their foliage occupy as little space as possible. Four or five more sticks are then to be tied firmly round the outside of the pot; and the whole may be enveloped in a sheet of paper. This being done, place the plants in the small box; pass some narrow strips of wood, which may be secured by nails from the outside, over the rims of the pots, to prevent the plants from being injured, if the box should upset; and fill the latter up firmly with carded wool, which has been previously warmed. After the lid is fastened down, the box must be placed within, and equidistant from the sides of the larger one, over the bottom of which a layer of dry moss should be previously placed; the space between the boxes to be tightly filled with the same material.

The lid of the large box may then be nailed down, and the whole wrapped up and corded in the woollen cloth.

Packed in this way, plants have been sent in mid-winter a journey in which they have been forty-eight hours on the road without their sustaining the least injury. Under ordinary circumstances, and for a journey of a few hours, the plants would, perhaps, pass uninjured in the small box, packed in wool, and wrapped in the woollen cloth; more especially if we could ensure its travelling "inside" the coach; but as coachmen are not to be trusted, it will not be advisable to run the risk with valuable plants. Wool, hair, or charcoal dust, would be superior to moss, to fill in between the boxes, but they would be more expensive. (*Gard. Chron.*, 1842. 805.)

*Dung beds, for fruiting*, are made in two forms, viz., so that the heat may be communicated direct to the earth in which the plants are growing, by this being placed upon the fermenting mass, or by there being a chamber beneath the earth to which the heat and steam are admitted from linings or coatings of dung with which it is surrounded. Both these systems labour under the disadvantage of having the heat, contrary to the course of nature, emanate from below, and thus placing the roots in a temperature as hot, or hotter, than that in which the leaves are vegetating.

The hotbed, for fruiting, must be of the largest size, being required to generate during the coldest season, a high degree of heat, and for a longer time than that devoted to raising seedlings.

A hotbed is usually made of stable-dung, of which that made by the best-fed horses is to be prefered.

It should be about ten days from the stalls, and without too large a proportion of litter. After being thrown into a heap, of conic form, for five or six days, it must be so turned over that the inner parts are brought to the outside, the clots well separated with the fork, the heap being reformed conical as before, and left for an equal number of days. By this time and treatment the dung in general acquires a sufficient and steady heat; if, however, it is very dry and fresh, it must be moderately moistened, and left for five or six days more. At the time of forming the heap, as well as at every turning, water should be applied if its substance appears at all dry, as a regular state of moisture is of first importance to the obtaining a favourable fermentation. It should remain until the straw in general assumes a dark brown colour, when it should be immediately formed into the bed. Leaves, or tan, may be mixed with advantage, as heat is thereby generated during a greater length of time. In cold, wet, or boisterous weather, the heaps should be covered to a moderate depth with litter.

The site of the bed being determined, a stake

should be placed perpendicularly at each of the four corners, as a guide for its rectangular construction. The dung must be thoroughly mixed just before it is used, and as carefully separated and spread regularly with the fork, as the bed is formed with it. It is beneficially settled down in every part alike by beating with the fork as the work proceeds, rather than by treading; for if too much compressed, a high degree of heat is generated, but is soon spent; a contrary phenomenon is often caused if trod to a still greater excess, namely, that no heat at all is engendered.

The longest or littery part of the dung should be laid at the bottom of the bed, and the finer fragments of the dung upon the top. If it is not regularly and moderately moist throughout, it should be sprinkled over with water. As the surface on which the bed is founded is usually horizontal, so is the dung laid perfectly parallel with it. Mr. Knight recommends it, on the contrary, to be equally inclined with its foundation, that it may associate well with the new form, which he recommends for frames.

The breadth of a bed must always be five feet, and in the depth of winter four and a half feet high when firmly settled; to form it of this size, about twelve barrow-loads of dung are required to a light.

In early spring, a height of three and a half feet is sufficient, and as the season advances, it may be reduced to three, or two and a half feet. In May, or early summer, when the only object is to hasten the germination of seeds, two feet or eighteen inches is not less than the necessary height. The length of the bed, in all cases, must be guided by the size of the frame.

To prevent the sudden changes of temperature in the external air affecting the heat of the bed, coat the sides of the bed with sand; coal-ashes, or earth, might be substituted, to a thickness of two feet.

As the heat declines, linings, or as they might be more properly called, coatings, are made use of, which consist of hot fermenting dung, laid from eighteen to twenty-four inches, in proportion to the coldness of the season, &c., all round the bed to the whole of its height, and if founded in a trench, one equally deep must be dug for the coating, it being of importance to renew the heat as much as possible throughout its whole mass; if, after a while, the temperature again declines, the old coating must be taken away, and a similar one of hot dung applied in its place. As the spring advances, the warmth of the sun will compensate for the decline of that of the bed; but as the nights are generally yet cold, either a moderate coating, about nine or ten inches thick, is required, or the mowings of grass, or even litter may be laid round the sides with advantage.

The depth of earth, as well as the time and manner

of applying, vary considerably; it should never be put on until four or five days after the bed is formed: before it is applied, the edges of the bed should be raised full eight inches higher than the middle, as from the additional weight of the frame they are sure to sink more and quicker, thereby often causing the earth to crack and injure the roots of the plants.

The roots of plants being liable to injury from an excessive heat in the bed, several plans have been devised to prevent this effect. If the plants in pots are plunged in the earth of the bed, they may be raised an inch or two from the bottom of the holes they are inserted in by means of a stone. But a still more effectual mode is to place them within other pots, rather larger than themselves; a space filled with air being thus interposed between the roots and the source of heat, an effectual security is obtained. To prevent the same injury occurring when the plants are in the earth of the bed, a moderate layer of neats-dung laid between the earth and the fermenting mass is an efficient precaution, and is much preferable to a similarly-placed layer of turf, which interrupts too much the full benefit of the heat. A plan recommended by Bradley is well worthy of notice. A woven hurdle, somewhat larger than the frame, being placed upon the dung, on this its woodwork can rest, and the earth is laid within it, thus the whole can be moved together without disturbance. This would especially be of advantage when bark is employed, which requires occasional stirring to renew its heat in case of emergency, when time cannot be allowed for the bed becoming regular in its heat before the plants are inserted. Besides these precautions, vacancies should be left in the mould, and holes bored with a thick pole into the bed, which must be filled up with hay or dung when the danger is passed.

For ascertaining the internal temperature of the bed, the thermometer is the only certain guide, as it also is for judging of the temperature of the air within the frame; the mode of introducing it into the body of the bed, is to have the thermometer inclosed in a wooden case of the size and form of an ordinary dibble, which is to be lined with baize and fitted with a cap of tinned iron to exclude the exterior temperature. The end which enters the earth is shod with perforated copper. In conjunction with the thermometer, trying sticks may be employed for occasional observation; these are smooth laths of wood, about two feet in length, thrust into different parts of the bed, which being drawn out and grasped quickly afford a rough estimate of the heat of the bed.

The small extent of the frame, and the rapid deterioration of the air within it by the plants, render its frequent renewal necessary. To effect this, the common practice is to raise the glasses in proportionate heights according to the state of the air; and to prevent any injury arising when necessarily admitted during inclement weather, mats ars hung over the opening; but notwithstanding these precautions, the supply of air can seldom be regular; hence, and from sudden chills, the plants are often checked, and sometimes essentially injured. It may be remarked here, that raw foggy days, if any thing, are more unfavourable than those that are frosty for the admission of air. A complete remedy for all these difficulties is afforded by a plan, which succeeds on the principle that warm air ascends, and simply consists of a pipe passed through the body of the bed, and one end communicating with the exterior air, the other opening into the frame, at one of the top corners, of which an aperture must be made; the heated air of the frame will constantly be issuing from this aperture, and its place supplied by that which rises through the pipe. A pipe of lead may be used, about two or three inches in diameter, bent nearly at a right angle, and each limb being three feet long, one of these to be placed horizontally as the bed is forming, with its mouth extending in the open air, that of the other opening into the frame; a cap should be fitted to the first, and by a slit on its under side, the quantity of air admitted can be regulated.

Although stable manure is generally employed for the constructing of hotbeds, yet there are several other vegetable matters that are also in use for the same purpose. Tanner's bark, from its long continuance and regularity of heat, is much to be prefered. In many situations it can be obtained at a cheaper rate than stable dung; it should be employed when fresh drawn from the vats, or at most when a fortnight or three weeks old; it must lay in a heap for six or eight days to allow the escape of the superfluous moisture: in summer this is not of such material consequence, as an excess of wet is, at this season, not so liable to prevent fermentation.

If the ground is dry, a pit three feet deep may be dug, and is better lined with slates, boards, or brick-work, but whatever may be the nature of the soil, it is best to form this case or bin of a similar height upon the surface. Without some support the tan will not form a solid bed, and if mould becomes mixed with it, the fermentation is retarded or entirely prevented. The breadth must not be less than five or six feet, or of a length shorter than ten or twelve, otherwise the heat will not be lasting. When the bark is laid, it must be gently settled with the fork, but never trodden upon; for if violently compressed, it loses the power of fermenting: if the bark is fresh and not ground very small, it attains a sufficient warmth in a fortnight for the insertion of the plants, and will continue in heat for two or three months; the larger the fragments of the bark are, the longer time it requires to ferment, but in an equal proportion it attains a higher temperature and preserves it much longer; a middle sized bark is, therefore, in general to be prefered; and added to the above consideration, it is to be remarked that, when made of large fragments, violent and sudden excesses often arise, even after the bed has been constructed two or three months: on the contrary, if very small the fermentation soon passes off.

When the crops are removed, and the heat declines, if well stirred, and a load or two of fresh bark mixed with it, the bed will acquire and continue in heat for an equal further lapse of time: this may be repeated throughout the year as often as the heat is found to decline. But it is necessary every autumn, entirely or nearly so, to reconstruct the bed with fresh bark; for when the old is far advanced towards putrefaction, it will no longer generate heat.

The leaves of the oak and sweet chesnut, and doubtless of many other trees, answer for hotbeds as well, or even better than tanner's bark, since they will continue to afford a moderate heat for nearly twelve months without any addition or stirring. They are to be collected as they fall in autumn, and carried to some situation, or be so hurdled in, that they may be preserved from scattering by the winds; the heap should be six or seven feet thick, trod firmly down, and moderately watered if dry. In a few days, a very powerful heat is produced, and in five or six weeks will have become so regular, that it may be broken up and the beds constructed with its materials, water being again employed if dryness appears, and they must be well trod down as before. There are many other substances that generate heat during fermentation; there is perhaps no vegetable substance that does not; even a heap of dry sticks acquires a strong accession of temperature if moistened. Mr. Burnet recommends the trial of the refuse matter thrown off in dressing flax, for constructing hotbeds: this refuse he says he has observed, when left undisturbed, continue at a temperature of 64 deg. for many months: he seems to intimate as long as fourteen. This material is, however, to be had in very few districts. Grass and other green herbage, and even wetted straw mixed with coal-ashes, have been used on an emergency with success. Instead of forming hotbeds with open sides, as has been hitherto described, *pits* of brickwork and other materials are very generally constructed for containing the fermenting mass. (*Johnson's Dict. Mod. Gard.* 324)

*Heating by Linings.* The following plan, suggested by Mr. W. Jones, has the great merits of simplicity and cheapness:

" In the first place measure the frame, and then dig a hole three feet deep, and sufficiently long and wide to admit of the frame standing two feet six inches clear of the sides all round, which space will be used for dung linings; then take some bundles of old pea-sticks, or any other coarse wood, cut the exact length or breadth of the box, and build up a stack of them in the middle of the hole to the height of four feet; lay some long litter on the top of this to prevent the soil mixing amongst the wood, and then place on the box; after which, lay about six inches of soil all over the surface inside, and press it well against the sides of the box, to prevent the steam from getting in and injuring the plants. Form a hill under the centre of each light to receive the plants, which may be put in as soon as the temperature has been raised to a sufficient degree, *i. e.* 75 or 80 degrees, by means of dung linings all round the sides. By this simple plan the gardener will have complete control over the bottom heat, which is a very essential point in keeping his plant in health and vigour: by turning the linings occasionally, he can regulate it from one end of the year to another with great facility. As the wood forms an air chamber underneath the soil, it will take less dung to keep up a proper temperature for two or three lights of cucumbers grown in this manner than any other. But previous to working dung into these linings, it should be allowed to ferment, and thus the rankest of the steam will pass off." (*United Gard. Journ.* 1846. 41.)

The chief advantage heating by linings has over the mode of having the dung directly beneath the soil of the bed, is the facility it affords to renewing the heat by fresh linings whenever requisite. On the other hand, linings are least economical of heat, this radiating perpendicularly more profusely than in any other direction. To check this, to confine its course more under the earth of the bed, and to keep the linings from being chilled by excessive rain, shutters to cover them during early forcing are necessary, particularly for the front linings, to throw off the water that falls on the lights. And they may be so constructed as to convey the water, falling on the lights, to the east and west corners of the pit, into a small drain, and thence to be conveyed away.

*The frames.* A one-light frame may be about four feet and a half in width from back to front, and three feet six inches the other way; fifteen or eighteen inches high in the back, and nine in front, with a glass sash or light, made to fit the top completely, to slide up and down, and move away occasionally.

The two-light frame may be seven feet long, four and a half wide, and fifteen or eighteen inches high in the back, with bars reaching from it at top to the front, serving both to strengthen the frame and help to support the lights; the two lights to be each three feet six inches wide, and made to fit the top of the frame exactly.

The three-light frames should be ten feet six inches long, four and a half wide, and from eighteen inches to two feet high in the back, and from nine to twelve or fifteen inches in front—observing that those designed principally for the culture of melons, may be rather deeper than for cucumbers, because they generally require a greater depth of earth on the beds; though frames, eighteen or twenty inches in the back, and from nine to twelve in front, are often made to serve occasionally, both for cucumbers and melons; each frame to have two cross-bars, ranging from the top of the back to that of the front, at three feet six inches distance, to strengthen the frame, and support the lights; and the three lights to be each three feet six inches wide; the whole together being made to fit the top of the frame exactly, every way in length and width.

Sometimes the above sort of frames are made of larger dimensions than before specified; but in respect to this it should be observed that if larger they are very inconvenient to move to different parts where occasionally wanted, and require more heat to warm the internal air: and in respect to depth particularly, that if they are but just deep enough to contain a due depth of mould, and for the plants to have moderate room to grow, they will be better than if deeper, as the plants will be then always near the glasses—which is an essential consideration in early forcing—and the internal air will be more effectually supported in a due temperature. For the deeper the frame, the heat of the internal air will be less in proportion, and the plants being far from the glasses will be disadvantageous in their early growth. Besides, a frame too deep, both in early and late forcing, is apt to draw the plants up weak; for they always naturally aspire towards the light, and the more space there is the more they will run up; for which reason the London kitchen gardeners have many of their frames not more than fourteen or fifteen inches high behind, and seven in front, especially those which are intended to winter the more tender plants, such as cauliflower and lettuce, and for raising early small salad herbs, radishes, &c.

The woodwork of the back, ends, and front, should be of inch or inch and a quarter deal, as before observed, which should be all neatly planed smooth on both sides; and the joints, in framing them together, should be so close that no wet nor air can enter. The cross-bars or bearers at top, for the support of the glasses, should be about three inches broad and one thick, and neatly dovetailed in at back and front even with both edges, that the lights may shut down close, each having a groove or channel along the middle to conduct off all wet falling between the lights. At the end of each frame, at top, should be a thin slip of board, four inches broad, up to the outside of the lights, to guard against cutting winds rushing in at that part immediately upon the plants, when the lights are occasionally tilted behind for the necessary admission of fresh air, &c.

With respect to the lights, the woodwork of the frame should be an inch and a half thick, and two and a half broad; and the bars for the immediate support of the glasswork should be about an inch broad, and not more than an inch and a half thick; for if too broad and thick, they would intercept the rays of the sun, so should be only just sufficient to support the lights, and be ranged from the back part to the front, eight or nine inches asunder.

All the woodwork, both of the frames and lights, should be painted to preserve them from decay. A lead colour will be the most eligible; and if done three times over, outside and in, will preserve the wood from the injuries of weather, and from the moisture of the earth and dung.

Mr. Knight has suggested an important improvement in the form of frames. He observes, that the general practice is to make the surface of the bed perfectly horizontal, and to give an inclination to the glass. That side of the frame which is to stand towards the north is made nearly as deep again as its opposite; so that if the mould is placed an equal depth (as it ought to be) over the whole bed, the plants are too far from the glass at one end of the frame and too near at the other. To remove this inconvenience, he points out the mode of forming the bed on an inclined plane ; and the frame formed with sides of equal depth, and so put together as to continue perpendicular when on the bed, as represented in the accompanying sketch.

For the winter forcing of cucumbers the angle of inclination of the ground should be much greater for the sake of obtaining more rays of solar light and heat during that season.

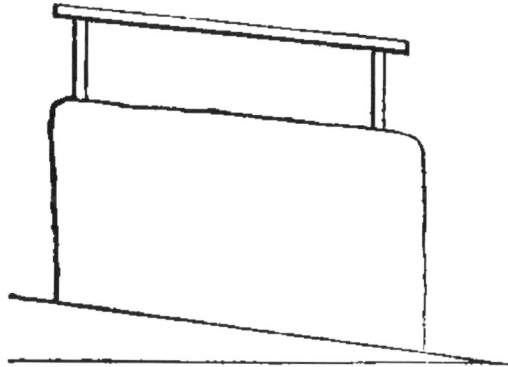

There are several minor points in the construction of frames that deserve attention. The strips of lead or wood that sustain the panes of glass should run across the frame, and not lengthways ; they then neither obstruct the light nor the passing off of rain. The inside of the frame should be painted white, since plants generally suffer in them for want of light ; if the accumulation of heat was the object in view, the inside colour should be black. *(Johnson's Dict. of Mod. Gard. 251.)*

*Pits,* though most expensive when first constructed,

fully repay for the outlay by the saving of labour, economy of heat, and greater certainty in the crops during after years, to say nothing of their superior neatness. The following are the best, and are the structures suggested and employed by some of the most successful of modern cucumber cultivators.

Mr. Flanaghan only allows the heat of fermenting dung to be employed, the steam being prevented entering the frame. One advantage arising from this he states to be, that fresh made dung may be employed, and consequently the loss sustained by any preparation is prevented. If, however, it be a fact that the steam of dung is rather beneficial than otherwise, fresh fermenting dung can be used without any detriment that I am aware of in other pits of which we have plans. Mr. F. describes his pit as follows :—It is four feet deep within, the lowest ten inches of solid brickwork sunk in the earth ; the remander is a flue three inches wide in the clear, carried entirely round the pit, the inner wall of which, forming the sides of the pit, is four inch work, well bedded in mortar, and pointed to prevent the steam penetrating ; the outer wall of the flue is also four inch, but open work to admit the steam, and that of dung coatings into the flue, the top of which is rendered tight by a covering of tiles, &c. The frame rests on the external wall of the flue. The cavity of the pit, which is kept dry by means of drains, is nine feet two inches long, two feet eight inches

wide, and four feet deep. It is filled with broken
bricks to within eighteen inches of the top, then a
foot of short cold dung, six inches of very rotten dung
trod down so as to admit half an inch depth of coal-
ashes, for preventing the intrusion of any worms that
may be in the dung, completes the structure.

The accompanying sketch and references will fully
explain the plan of Mr. West. D D, chamber in
which the dung is
placed, three and a half
feet deep, surrounded
by 9-inch brickwork.
One half of this is filled
longitudinally with
dung at the commence-
ment, which, if kept close shut up, will last twelve or
eighteen days, according to the quality of the dung.
As the heat declines, the other side is filled, and the
temperature is further sustained by additions to the
top of both as the mass settles. When this united
heat becomes insufficient, the side first filled being
cleared, the old manure must be mixed with some
fresh, and replaced, this being repeated alternately to
either heap as often as necessary. A A, are the doors,
two of which are on each side for the admission of the
dung. They are two and a half feet square, fitted
into grooves at the bottom, and fastened by means of
a pin and staple at the top. B B, are small areas

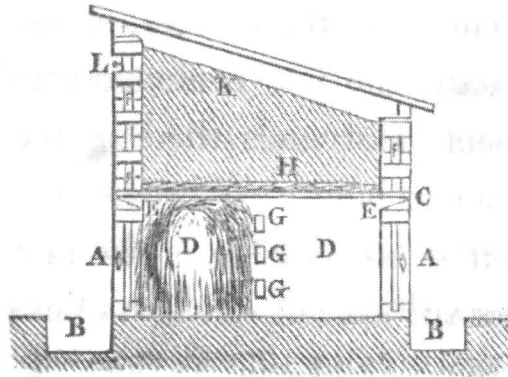

sunk in front, surrounded by a curb of wood ; G G G, are bars passing longitudinally as a guide and support in packing the dung ; c, represents a bar of cast-iron, two inches wide and three-quarters of an inch thick, placed on the edge of which there is a row, a foot asunder, across the chamber, to support a layer of wood branches and leaves, H, for the purpose o sustaining the soil, K, in the upper chamber ; E E, represents the orifices, of which there are a series all round the pit, communicating with the flue F F F, which surrounds the beds ; the exterior wall of this flue is built with bricks laid flat, the inner one of bricks set on edge. The flue is two inches wide, and for the sake of strength bricks are passed occasionally from side to side as ties. The top of the flue, and the internal part of the wall, which rises at the back and front to the level the earth is meant to stand, are covered with tiles, over the joints of which slips of slate bedded in mortar are laid to prevent the escape of the steam of the dung. L, represents one of two plugs, with stop holes left to regulate the heat and steam as may be necessary. The outer wall supports the lights. For the convenience of fixing the dung, it is best to fill the half of the chamber at the commencement, before the branches, mould, &c., are put in. (*Johnson's Dict. Mod. Gard.*)

Mr. John Mearns, gardener to William Harbing, Esq., at Shopden Court, near Leominster, grows early cucumbers in a pit the walls of which (*a*) are of open

wicker - work
There is a cavity
under the bed
(*c*) into which
the steam from
the dung lining
is admitted;
posts of iron or
stone (*b*) support

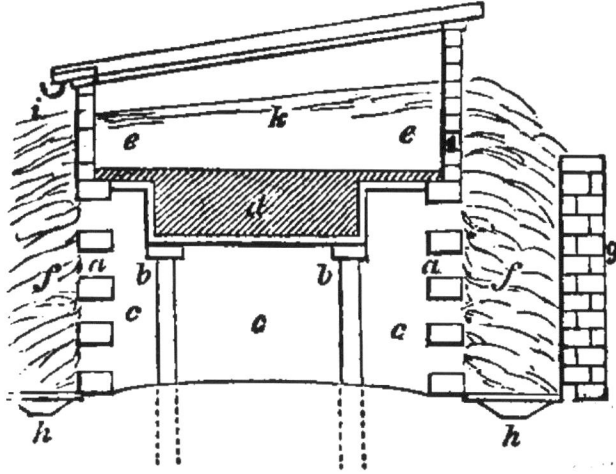

this bed (*d*), which is made of slate, stones, or tiles;
while the cavity between, and the sides of the pit, are
closed below with slabs of stone (*e*). The pit is
heated by dung linings (*f*), inclosed by walls (*g*),
and kept dry by drains (*h*), and by a gutter to the
sashes (*i*). The plants are inserted in a hill, and
gradually earthed up in the usual manner. This pit
is much cheaper than Mc.Phail's, especially if the
retaining walls (*g*) are omitted. (*Gard. Mag.* i.
170.)

Mr. Mills' pit, heated by fermenting dung without
admitting the vapour and gases from it to communi-
cate with the plants, is constructed as follows:—
A, nine-inch walls inclosing dung linings; B, cavities
to be filled with linings; C, five courses of four-inch
work pigeon-holed; D, cavity in chamber filled with
heated air; E, brick-on-edge partition excluding fumes
of the dung; G, frame; H, trellis for training plants

on; I, earth for planting in; J, cavity filled with

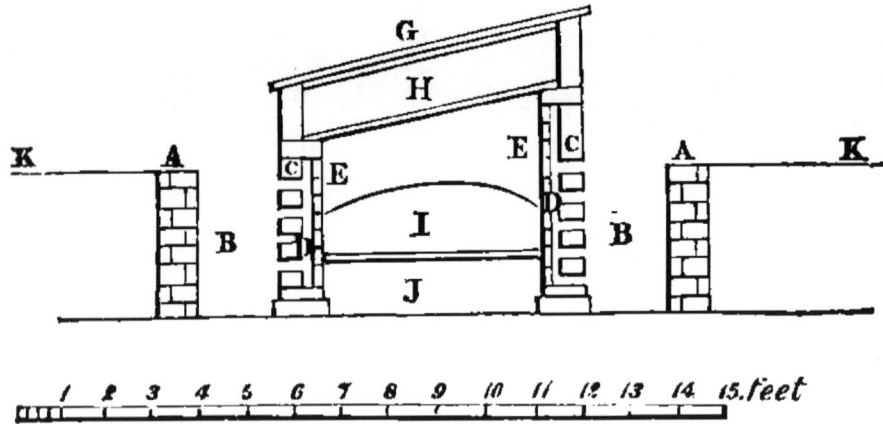

large wood; K, ground level. (*Mills' Treatise on Culture of Cucumber*, 1.)

Instead of dung, even in Flannagan's and Mearns' pits, *bark* might be employed as a source of heat, but in the following system, practised by Mr. Barton, the gardener at Springfield, near Liverpool, bark is especially used in conjunction with fire heat. The pit is 48 feet in length by 10 feet wide, heated by a common flue. A bark bed, of four feet wide, is filled to two and a half feet with fresh tanner's bark; upon this a thin layer of rotten dung is placed, upon which is put a layer of the top spit of a piece of pasture land, broken fine with the spade. This brings the surface of the bed to about two feet from the roof of the pit. The plants are fastened to stakes till they reach a trellis which is fixed six inches from the glass, and upon which they are trained. Mr. Barton commences forcing the latter end of January, and very little air is given during the growth of the plants. If it is found requisite to admit air, it is done early in the fore part of the day. The temperature is made to range from 75 to 80 degrees, as near as practicable, and the plants are syringed early in the morning and again in the afternoon. By this method fruit are cut by the first week in April. (*Gard. Chron.* 1843. 336.)

*Fire heat*, unassisted by fermenting bark, may be employed to maintain the requisite temperature; and the following plan is as simple as it is economical, requiring only an excavation 2½ feet deep, and of the length and breadth of the frame, to be first dug out; in this a flue of brick or any other material is carried along, nearly on one side of the pit, from a furnace at one end, and returns on the other to a chimney carried up over the fire-place. Posts are driven at the corners, and intermediate ones at the back and front. On these posts is laid a stage of wattled (*i. e.* wicker-work) hurdles, closely enough woven to prevent the mould of the bed from falling through. (*Gard. Mag.* iv. 362.)

On this platform a frame of sufficient depth is placed, and within this a bed of suitable compost, 18 inches thick, is put for the plants. By this trifling structure and simple means, a perfect command of heat is obtained, at very little expense; and where proper skill is applied, and the necessary degree of moisture is obtained, in connection with the fire heat, there is no doubt of a successful result. When the required heat (70 degrees) is found in the frame, a damper, fitted at the bottom of the upright chimney, is shut, thereby confining the heat in the flue and heat chamber, which is further regulated by ordinary coverings. (*Ibid.*)

*Hot water* is now very frequently employed as a source of heat, and I think it is much more manageable than any other, though more expensive than dung, for the same purpose. It may be applied by mean's of pipes or a tank.

*Pipes.* The following is the pit employed by Mr. Mitchell, at Worsley Gardens, and secures these four desirable objects: 1. A circulation of air without loss of heat. 2. The command of a supply of moisture proportioned to the temperature. 3. The desired amount of bottom heat. 4. The necessary supply of external air without producing a cold draught. The method by which the first of these is secured will be understood by refering to the section annexed, in which *a* is the flow pipe, *b b b* the return pipes in the chamber A. It is evident that as the air in the chamber becomes heated it will escape upwards by the opening near *a*, and the cold air from the passage B will rush in to supply its place; but the ascending current of heated air coming in contact with the glass is cooled, descends, and entering the passage B, passes into the chamber A, where it is again heated; and thus a constant circulation is produced. In order to obtain the second object, to some extent the tank and pipe systems are combined. The flow pipe *a* is put half its diameter into the channel c, which, when filled with water (or so far as is necessary), gives off a vapour exactly proportionable to the heat of the pipe and pit.

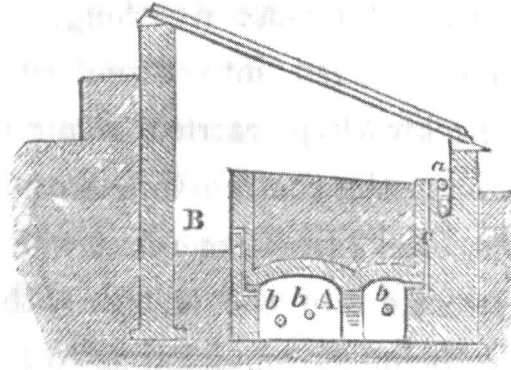

The third requisition is produced by the surrounding atmosphere and heating materials. The fourth is accomplished simply by lowering the upper sash; the cold air thus entering at the top only, falls directly into the passage B, and passes through the hot chamber before coming in contact with the plants. In order to test the circulation, a piece of paper, fixed near the front of the pit, shewed the current to be so strong as to bend it backwards, and give it a tremulous motion. When the heat in the chamber is 95 deg., in the open space over the bed it is 71 deg.; in the bottom of the passage only 60 deg.; and in the mould in the bed it is 80 deg. (*Ibid.*)

*Tank.* This has the advantage over pipes of retaining its heat through the night better; but the combination of the two is, perhaps, the best which has been suggested. It was designed, and is employed, by Mr. Green, gardener to Sir E. Antrobus.

The construction of the pit is as follows:—the walls are built of 9-inch brickwork, five feet in the back, and two and a half in the front, and five feet wide in the clear, thirty-six feet long, covered with nine lights, and divided into three compartments. A trough of brickwork is carried along the bottom from end to end in the centre; this is constructed by first laying two bricks thick one foot wide, and then forming the two sides of the trough with bricks on edge, the whole being so cemented as to hold water.

The pit is heated with hot water by means of a branch of two and a half inch pipes proceeding from the boiler, which heats a stove at a short distance. The hot water flows along the back and front of the pit, but the return pipes are placed in the trough first described, which is filled with water, or partly so, as circumstances may require, by means of a small pipe that leads to the outside. Another small pipe is laid in the bottom of the trough for letting off the stagnant water, and for emptying it occasionally; for in very dark damp weather a drier heat is required.

The soil that Mr. Green uses, is collected at least six months before it is wanted for use, and consists of turf, not more than three inches thick, of strong maiden loam, built up in narrow ridges, with a layer alternately of an equal quantity of fresh horse-dung, and a good portion of straw. When wanted for use it is chopped up with a spade, is not sifted, and one-third of well-decayed leaf mould is added.

In order to have a succession of fruit, Mr. Green sows the seed at three different times, the 1st and 20th of September, and the 5th of November. The plants of the first and second sowing are fruited in No. 2 pots, and of the third are planted out. In placing the plants in the fruiting pots, a quantity of large potsherds are put at the bottom, with some large pieces of turf and dung, in order to insure a good drainage. The plants are put sufficiently deep to leave three or four inches of the top of the pot, so that the plants may be earthed up as they advance in growth. When the pots are filled with roots, a good supply of water is given, of the same temperature as that of the air they are grown in.

One plant is placed in the centre of each light, care being taken that the bottom of each pot is about four inches above the water in the trough and the return pipe. The branches are trained on a temporary trellis, and the fruit is allowed to hang down. From the plants sown on the 1st of September, the first fruit is cut in the first week of November; from that date to the 4th of December, it is not unusual to cut from three lights, or three plants, forty cucumbers **of** the Sion House kind, varying from twelve to fifteen inches in length. The same plants will continue bearing till about Christmas. The plants of the **first** sowing are thrown away at Christmas, and plants **of** the third sowing are planted out in their place. **The** plants of the second sowing are productive from December until March ends. When the plants **are** grown in a bed, Mr. Green forms the bottom of it **by** laying some strong stakes across the trough, **and** covering them with any rough boards. The stakes so laid will leave a cavity round the back and front of the trough, so as to allow the heat and moisture **to** rise. The plants are put on a narrow ridge, **and** earthed up in the usual way as they advance in growth, and the branches are trained upon a trellis, in the same way as for the plants in pots. These plants will bear well through the spring and summer months.

As soon as the first three lights can be spared, **Mr.** Green introduces shelves fifteen inches from **the** glass, and fills them with strawberry plants, and the pit answers equally well for them as for cucumbers; only for strawberries the water in the trough requires to be stopped off, which is done by means of a stuffing-box. The plants, of course, require **a** great quantity of air both night and day at first.

The advantages gained by this pit are **a** great

saving of labour and dung, which last, at all times, makes a very littery and unsightly appearance ; the having a sufficient command of heat in severe and changeable weather, and the return pipe being buried, or partly buried in water, gives, when required, a sufficient bottom heat; and the constant vapour arising from it renders the plants so healthy and strong, that a good crop of fine fruit is certain. (*Gard. Chron.* 1841.  36.)

The following are the plans of pits invented respectively, by Mr. Cobbett, of Pencarrow, and Mr. Green.  The first being heated by open troughs containing the hot water :—

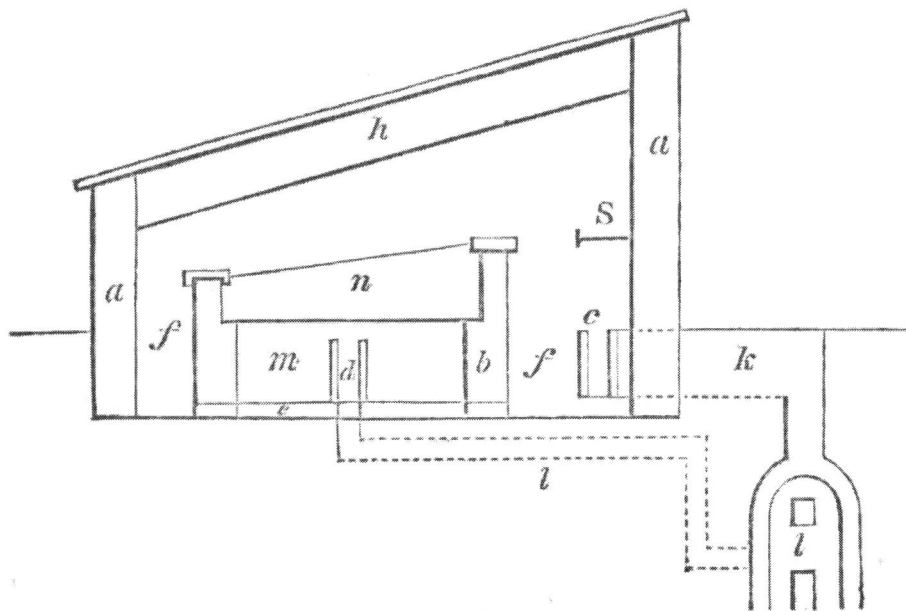

*a*, Walls of pit ; *b*, walls of bed ; *c*, trough for heating air of the pit ; *d*, trough under the soil, in the air tight chamber *m* ; resting on the openings *e*, for conveying the cooled air from the front walk to the trough *c* to be heated; *f*, walks; *S*, shelf for plants; *h*, trellis for the cucumber vines; *i*, return pipe for the hot water; *k*, the trough, at entering the pit it is closed; *l*, Shewin's conical boiler; *n*, soil for cucumber roots. (*Duncan's Culture of the Cucumber*, 22.)

GREEN'S PIT.

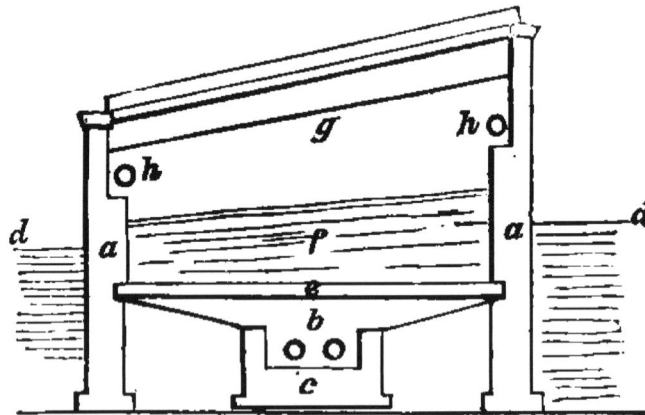

*Scale, 1-6th of an inch to the foot.*

*a a*, outer walls; *b*, hot water pipes, in a brick trough, *c*; *d d*, ground level; *e*, joists, forming floor of pit; *f*, bed for planting or plunging; pipes may pass up through this, to admit moist air as required from the chamber below; *g*, the trellis; *h h*, hot water pipes for top heat. (*Suburban Gardener*, 506.)

Mr. Cuthill, florist, of Camberwell, very justly adverts to the ill consequences of building brick pits for cucumbers, &c., later than July or August, lest the mortar should not be thoroughly dried. If this is not attended to, the mortar, when heated by dung, will often emit a noxious vapour that destroys the young plants. Mr. Cuthill strongly recommends solid sides to brick pits, instead of pigeon holes, because he is able to apply hot fresh dung immediately to the walls in the former case, and in the latter it is necessary to sweeten it. He states, that in such pits his early melons, sown on the 1st of Feruary, have been cut in the first week of May. In winter, for cucumbers, he thinks no plan equal to Mr. Green's. (*Gard. Chron.*, 1841. 150.)

*Stove Culture* is the most elegant, most certain, and least troublesome, for growing the cucumber in perfection.

Mr. Ayres has erected a stove devoted to its cultivation, and, as for this purpose it is most desirable to obtain the greatest amount of solar influence during the winter months, he has the glass placed at an angle, much nearer to a right angle than is usually employed for the cucumber pits or frames. He has selected the angle of 51 degrees, but I think that from 55 to 61 degrees would be even preferable.

The following is a sketch of Mr. Ayres' stove, on a scale of a quarter of an inch to the foot : *a*, is the tan-bed, in which the pots containing the plants are plunged ; *b*, is the trellis to which the plants are trained ; *c*, is the pathway, under which is a flue, with the pipe of an Arnott's **stove passing** through it; and *d*, is the ground line.

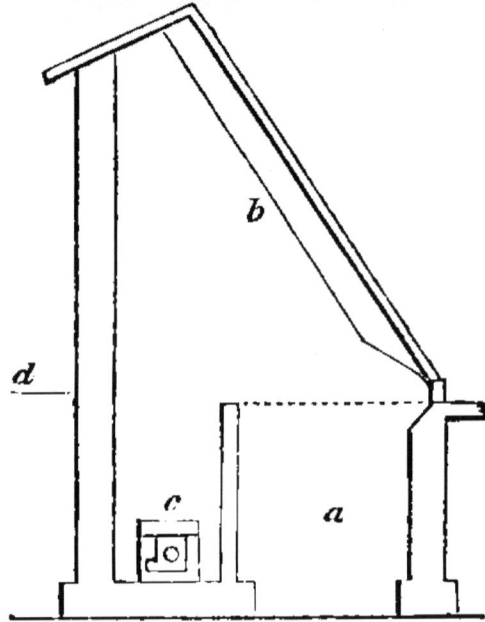

The Arnott's stove must stand in a vault, accessible from without, about a foot below the level of the bottom of the flue, to secure a good draught to the fire. The flue should be divided into four compartments, the first and third of which, by keeping the pipes wholly, or partially immersed in water, might be made to produce moist heat, while the others will produce dry heat; so that by tilting or removing the covering tiles of any of the compartments, the humidity of the atmosphere will be placed quite under the command of the attendant. The cost of the stove and piping to heat a house of the above dimensions, and twenty feet long, would be no more than £4 10s., and in the most severe weather, with the assistance of the bark bed, it would maintain a temperature of 65 or 70 degrees for about sixpence per . day; and in ordinary weather, it would not cost more than from eighteenpence to two shillings per week. A stove of this kind, with Welsh coal, would not require attending more than four times in twenty-four hours.

Mr. Ayres uses, turfy loam, two parts; thoroughly decomposed dung, two parts; leaf mould, two parts; and very sandy turfy peat, two, but not sifted. Manure water is prepared by steeping two pecks of sheep or deer dung, one peck of pigeon's dung, and a half a peck of soot, in a hogshead of boiling rain water, and used, alternately, with clear water from March to October. The great secret of keeping the cucumber in vigorous growth in pots, Mr. Ayres conceives, is the use of manure water. The plants should be raised from seed sown on the 1st of August, so as to be fit for planting, in fruiting pots, in the first week of September. These pots should not be less than sixteen inches wide, and eighteen inches deep. Two plants to be placed in each pot, but the leading shoot must not be stopped, but allowed to grow until it reaches to the top of the house. On this, success in pot culture mainly depends, for if the plants are stopped, they are thrown into a bearing state before they are sufficiently established, and the consequence is, early fruit, but a short-lived plant; but if the plants are allowed to grow to the length of ten or fifteen feet before the leading shoot is stopped, a great quantity of true sap will be generated, and the plant, consequently, will be better able to support a crop than if it had been allowed to bear fruit before it was properly established (p. 12). The temperature which Mr. Ayres approves of, is 60 degrees throughout the night, 65 degrees in dull, and 70 degrees in clear weather, by fire heat; and 80, 90, or even 100 degrees, with plenty of atmospheric moisture and air, in sunny weather. The two shoots from the two plants in each pot are to be trained to the trellis, at one foot nine inches apart; and when they begin to send out laterals, these must be stopped at one joint above the fruit. (*Ayres' Cucumber Culture in Pots*, 4, 12.)

Instead of employing pots, it would be a better plan to plant in earth, resting upon the tan, or with a moveable bottom between. The roots would thus have more room for their roots to pasture in.

Mr. T. Moore, one of the most scientific, and yet practical, gardeners of the present time, has suggested the following improved form and mode of heating the cucumber stove by hot water. He has also adopted the plan of growing without pot-culture.

"The house should be provided with a tank near the front, in which a circulation of heated water would supply a genial warmth to the soil and the roots: attached to the same boiler which heated the water in this tank, a series of pipes might be so arranged as

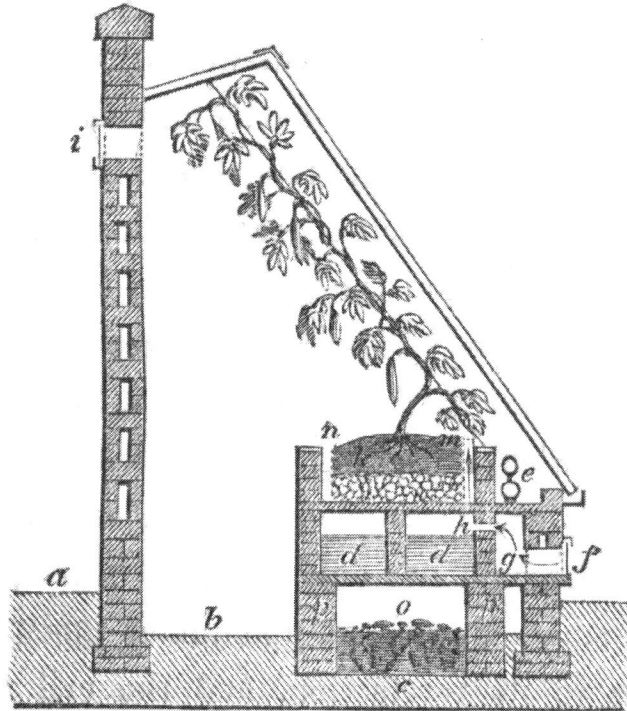

*a*, Ground level. *b*, Pathway. *c*, Lowest point excavated, on which a bed (*o*) may be made for rhubarb, &c. *d*, Tank, supported by brick piers (*p*). *e*, Pipes for the supply of atmospheric heat. *f*, Apertures for the admission of air, which passes through the chamber *g*, into the tank, by a series of openings at *h*, and thence into the house by the tubes *m*, escaping through the ventilators *i*. *m*, Bed of soil on which the plants grow.

to supply heat to the atmosphere above the tank, which should be constructed so as to be as near the glass as circumstances would admit: a shallow bed of soil to be placed, resting on a due portion of open rubble for drainage; the upper surface of the tank rendered level, so as to admit of water being poured in quantity among the loose drainage, which would ultimately, by the agency of the heat below, be induced to raise among the soil in the form of vapour, and thus duly to supply it with moisture. Beneath the tank, an open space would admit of mushrooms or rhubarb, &c., being cultivated with facility. The admission of air would be provided for by apertures through the front wall, communicating with the upper part of the tank above the level of the water; from thence small tubes would rise at intervals through the soil into the house, and this might be opened or closed at pleasure; the outer orifice would be provided with small sliding shutters, to exclude the external air when not required. By this arrangement the cold air would pass over the surface of the heated water, and become not only warmed in its progress, but also supplied with an amount of moisture proportionate to its rarefaction, and the evil resulting from the admission of cold dry air will thus be altogether prevented.

The plants are to be trained on a trellis placed about 15 inches from the glass, and their roots confined to certain portions of soil, which should from time to time be replenished. This might easily be accomplished by various arrangements; a few slates placed about each plant would serve as one simple means of effecting it. Transverse divisions must be introduced so as to allow of the removal and renewal of a plant and its soil without disturbing its neighbours; a complete succession might thus be effected. The structure itself would exteriorly be protected with shutters of light frame-work, covered with painted or tarred canvass. These should be kept about six inches from the glass, and thus a cavity would be formed, the air contained in which would serve to prevent that incessant drain upon the temperature of the house which takes place either when the covering is in contact with the glass or when altogether absent.

Next in importance and usefulness to a house such as is described, Mr. Moore recommends a pit heated in a similar manner, as being equally suited to accomplish the end in view, though somewhat less convenient in its application to practice. The principal difference between the house already referred to and such a pit would be the omission of the pathway at the back; and that the tank would occupy the whole width of the pit, except, perhaps, a cavity of six inches on either side, or else (which would be equally effectual) the improvement already described in this work might be adopted. The plants would be trained on a trellis near the glass, and be grown in shallow beds of soil above the tank. (*Flor. Journ. and Gard. Record,* 1845. 49.)

Mr. Moore gives the following directions for training in a house :—The plants being intended to occupy a surface of trellis-work in a line nearly parallel with the glass, it will be requisite to train their primary shoots to a sufficient length to reach from the soil to the trellis, before they are what is technically called ' stopped ;' this operation, by removing the central bud, or axis of development, induces the buds which are latently formed at the nodes of the branches to push forth and become the axis of further extension. Two or three of the strongest of these lateral shoots, situate towards the top of the stem, should be retained, and trained on the trellis in a direction towards the top of the house : these shoots should be placed about 18 inches from each other, and when they reached about one-third of the length of the trellis they also should be stopped, and thus several more lateral shoots will be produced. The uppermost strong shoot should in each case be still trained in the same upward direction, and the others must be disposed in the most convenient form in the space between the main branches : these, that is the growing lateral shoots, if they do not show a fruit blossom at the second joint or leaf from the main branch, must be stopped, and the young shoot thus induced to push forth will in all probability have fruit at the first leaf; if not, it must be stopped at every leaf as it extends, until fruit is observed. The upper portion of the branch, after having extended about one-third further up the roof, should be submitted to the same process ; and this must be again repeated until the whole of the trellis is covered. No reference has yet been made to the treatment of those lateral branches where the young fruit are perceived : these should be permitted to grow until the blossoms have expanded; and then, after this, they should be stopped at the leaf next beyond the fruit blossoms. By permitting them to grow until the flowers have expanded, the attraction of the growing branch will continue to draw up a regular supply of nutriment, part of which will be devoted in its course to assist the development of the blossoms; and besides the advantage of the growing point acting thus as a sucker to draw onwards the vital juices towards the young fruit, it will act also as an outlet to draw off what would otherwise be superabundant and dangerous to these tender organs of reproduction. (*Moore's Theory and Practice of Cucumber Culture*, 33.)

The following are also useful suggestions :

Let the house be constructed as follows : The back wall 9 feet high, and the front 4, above the ground level; a door as near the back wall as possible, and at one end of the house; the inside to be 10 feet wide, and heated with large flat hot-water pipes, cast with dishes on their upper surface for holding water. Let boxes be made 3 feet long, 14 inches deep, and 16 inches wide: the house will hold two rows of such boxes. In placing them where they are finally to remain, be careful to place them at a sufficient distance from the glass to admit of watering the root and adding fresh soil. Seeds sown on the 1st of August will produce plants to bear during November, December, and January; for plants to succeed these, sow on the 1st of September; these plants should not be allowed to bear till the beginning of February. The soil to be light fibrous loam; add to this one-fourth of leaf-mould and rotten dung, of equal parts; place large potsherds over the holes in the bottom of the box; above the potsherds a layer of turf. Make a small hill in the centre of each box; place one plant in the centre, and continue to add soil as the roots appear on the surface, taking care not to fill the box with soil till the plants are in full bearing. Water with manure water, occasionally with a little soot mixed with it. A temperature of 65 to 70 degrees by night, and 70 to 85 degrees by day (with assistance of sun), during winter. If the plants should flag about noon, as they frequently will during sunshine, sprinkle them with water immediately over the leaves; and as the spring advances, shade them lightly during the middle part of the day. Be careful to maintain a moist atmosphere by vapour from the pipes and frequent syringing; at the same time guard against over-watering the roots. To banish green-fly, use tobacco-water applied with the syringe; let it remain on the plants 20 minutes; afterwards syringe the plants with clean water. Give air every opportunity, but do not admit any in front of the house in cold weather. Plants under the above treatment have been kept in a bearing state for twelve months from seed sown on the 1st of September. (*Gard. Chron.* 1841. 117.)

Although a stove purposely erected for cucumber culture is to be prefered, yet it is not essential for its success. Mr. James Reed, of Bristol, employed a house built for grapes. This vinery was 40 feet long, 16 feet broad, 12 feet high at the back, and 5½ feet high in the front; with one fireplace, and a flue which passed round the house. The air could be admitted both by the top and front lights. On or about the 20th of September, cucumber seeds were sown on a moderate hotbed in the open air, and treated in the usual manner till they were ready to ridge out. This generally happened about the beginning of November, at which time the shoots of the vines were withdrawn from the house, and a dung-bed formed on the floor in the usual way. After placing the frame and earth on the bed, it may be left without the lights till the rank steam has passed off; and the plants being placed in the hills, and the sashes put on, the following are the leading features of management during the winter: Make fires in the evening, so as to warm the air of the house to from 56 to 60 degs., and in very severe frosts it may be raised to 70 degs. In the mornings of the coldest weather and shortest days make a strong fire, so as to raise the heat to nearly 70 degs. when the house is shut up. About eight o'clock, and from that time to half-past nine, give plenty of fresh air, by opening the front sashes and top lights; after which, and during the remainder of the day, give plenty of air to the cucumbers, by tilting the sashes in the usual way. In mild weather, and during sunshine, the lights may be taken entirely off for some hours each day; and, immediately after forming new linings, the top lights may be left down a little all night, to permit the escape of rank steam. The advantage of this mode of growing cucumbers during winter is the comparative certainty of an early and good crop, at one-third of the trouble and expense of the common method out of doors. By this practice, fruit may be cut in January. The vines may be introduced in the beginning of March, and will break regularly in consequence of the genial steam of the dung. In April, the shade of the vine leaves will have rendered the house too dark for the culture of the cucumber; and as, by this time, cucumbers are plentiful in the common hotbeds out of doors, the bed in the house may be cleared out, and the vines treated in the usual way till the following November. (*Gard. Mag.*, iii. 23.)

Cucumbers may be grown, according to the foregoing plan, in a peach-house, as well as in the vinery.

Mr. Duncan says, that in cucumber houses there should be shelves exclusively devoted for pots or boxes, near the glass, in the immediate influence of the sun's power.

In stoves, or vineries, or any other house, where cucumbers are grown in winter, there should be a similar contrivance; but in those periods of the year not directly winter, it does not so much signify where they are placed, so that they enjoy the influence of light, and proximity to the glass.

It is further evident, that cucumbers may be grown, in the summer, in the green house, especially such sorts as are extremely valuable, and when other convenience is deficient.

The usual temperature required for annuals, such as balsams, cockscombs, &c., is quite sufficient for the growth of cucumbers during a considerable period of the year. (*Duncan's Culture of Cucumber*, 76.)

---

## GENERAL CULTURE.

*Earthing the Beds.*—When the earth is put on for frame culture, it is at first to be spread only two or three inches deep, but under the centre of each light a hillock must be constructed, eight or ten inches deep and a foot in diameter. The earthing should be performed at least four or five days before planting, at which time the earth must be examined; if it be of a white colour and caked, or, as it is technically termed, burnt, it must be renewed, for the plants will not thrive in it, and holes bored in the bed to give vent to the steam.

The mould of the hillocks being well stirred, the plants must be turned out of the pots without disturbing the ball of earth, and one containing three plants inserted in each ; a little water previously heated to the requisite temperature must be given, and the glasses kept perfectly close until the next morning. Any plants not in pots must be moved by the trowel with as much earth pertaining to their roots as possible. The shade of a mat is always requisite during the meridian of bright days until the plants are well established. They must be pressed gradually away from each other, until at least eight inches apart ; nothing can be more erroneous than to allow them to proceed with the stems nearly touching.

When well taken root, earth must be added regularly over the bed, until it is level with the tops of the mounds ; for if there be not a sufficient depth of soil, the leaves will always droop during hot days, unless they are shaded, or more water given them than is proper.

*Pruning and Training.*—An important operation for the obtaining early fruit, but by no means so necessary for later crops, is the first pruning, or as it is termed, *stopping* the plant, that is, nipping off the top of the first advancing runner, which is to be done as soon as the plant has attained four rough leaves : this prevents its attaining a straggling growth, and compels it at once to shoot out laterals, which are the fruitful branches.

Mr. Duncan's directions relative to stopping are very judicious. He says, in November and December, while the influence of the sun is little, and the excitability of the vital principal feeble, the attempt to stop or interfere with the organism of the living plant should not be made, unless there is good proof that other shoots will be emitted at the axils of the ones stopped. But plants in a young state, in spring, should be stopped at the first joint from the cotyledon, and afterwards at the second. Their being fruitful or otherwise in the early part of their life, will depend in a great measure upon a proper performance of this operation. Plants intended for trellis culture should not be stopped until they have attained to a proper height, the distance from the soil of the bed to the trellis being necessary. The terminal bud, and every one below the three top ones, should be removed, and the shoots emitted from these will become the skeleton of the future system of branches. The tendency to elongate being invariable, should be as constantly directed to foreseen circumstances, maintaining a healthy vigour, and fine and abundant fruit, both in accordance with the known princip'es of vegetable physiology. Every useless or not required bud should be rubbed out immediately it is evolved, and every shoot superfluous or unnecessary removed with the fingers, the knife being required only in removing a denuded or worn out branch in a later age of being, and to cut the fruit. The shoots with fruit should be stopped at the second joint beyond, as soon as the fruit is out of bloom. The shoot emitted at the fruit, and the one before it, must be rubbed away; and should there be one behind it, that should be stopped, not removed; but the shoots emitted at the terminal bud, and others on other parts of the plants, must be encouraged to proceed unstopped to succeed in a similar way, proportioning their number and the number of fruit to the powers of vital excitement and extent of elaborating organs, not taking into calculation the decaying foliage. (*Duncan's Culture of the Cucumber*, 41.)

When the plants begin to run, if a trellis is not used, the shoots must be trained and pegged down at regular distances, which not only prevents their rubbing against the glass, but also becoming entangled with each other. Never more than two or three main branches should be left to each plant, all others to be removed as they appear. If more are left it causes the whole to be weak, and entirely prevents the due exposure of the foliage to the sun.

For attaining this last named object, as well as to obtain fruit unstained and of a uniform colour, it is by far the most preferable mode of training to have the branches supported on a wire trellis at a regulated and equal distance from the glass.

To promote the admission of light in fine days in winter, says Mr. Duncan, when it is calm it is very beneficial to clean the inside of the frame, by washing and wiping, using a little warm water and a sponge, and once a fortnight, or as often as required, the lights too ; these must be removed to a distance, and well syringed and washed with a soft brush; and before they are put on again allowed to dry.

While this is being done some other lights must be put on in their stead; but preferably to this, if it be convenient, is to use two sets of lights, one to be at rest and the other in use alternately every fortnight or three weeks. (*Ibid.* 54.)

The training must be regularly attended to, and all superabundance of shoots and leaves removed. If the plants which have been once stopped have extended their runners to three joints without showing fruit, they must be again stopped.

As the fruit advances, if not trained on a trellis, tiles, sand, or other material must be placed beneath it to preserve it from specking, or a glass cylinder is still better; if a bulb containing water is attached, the fruit grows faster and finer.

*Temperature and Ventilation.* The greatest care is necessary in regulating the temperature; it must never be allowed to decline below 70 deg. or rise above 95 deg. The temperature of the bed, as well as of the exterior air, governs also the degree of freedom with which the air may be admitted; whenever allowable, the glasses should be raised. The best time for doing so, is from ten to three o'clock.

It may not be misplaced to remark, that chilly, foggy days are even less propitious for admitting air than severe frosty ones; during such it is best to keep the frames close, and to lessen the opening of the glasses, in proportion as the air is cold or the beds declining, it never exceeding two inches under the most favourable circumstances. (*Johnson's Mod. Gard. Dict.*)

The following is the best mode of keeping up a current of warm dry air through the frame. This not only increases the health of the plants, but diminishes greatly that condensation of moisture on the glass, which is so prejudicial, and renders the raising of the lights unnecessary, except in the most favourable times. The plan was originally proposed by the celebrated vegetable physiologist, Dr. Hales. (*Lewis's Newman's Chem.* i. 411.) The mode succeeds on the principle that warm air ascends; and this is secured by a pipe passed through the body of the bed, or other source of heat, one of its apertures communicating with the exterior air, and the other opening into the frame; at one of the top corners of which an aperture or pipe, with a cap to close it when necessary, must be made ; the damp heated air of the frame constantly issues through this aperture, and its place is supplied by that which rises through the pipe. This suggestion was adopted by Mr. Keith, of Ravelstone, who states that he employs a leaden pipe of two or three inches diameter, bent nearly at a right angle, each limb being three feet long. One limb is placed horizontally in the body of the bed as it is forming, with the pipe's mouth extending in the open air, the other mouth opening into the frame. A cap should be fitted to the outside mouth, and if there be a slit in the side of the cap, (to be kept downwards when used,) the quantity of air admitted can be regulated. (*Mem. Caled. Hort. Soc.* iii. 185.)

Towards the conclusion of the first production of fruit in dung beds, it is a good practice to renew the heat by adding eighteen inches of fermenting dung all round the beds, previous coatings being entirely removed, and to earth over it to the same depth as in the interior of the bed. This prevents the roots, when they have extended themselves to the sides of the bed, being dried by exposure to the air and sun.

The fullest and most practical directions for the management of linings has been published by Mr. G. Mills. He says, linings should be turned over once in eight or ten days, to keep them in a regular state of fermentation, especially from November to February inclusive. They should not, however, be all turned at once; and if the back lining is turned, we will suppose, on the first or second, the frontage should be done on the fifth or sixth; so that one-half is turned in five days. The ends will not require turning so often, provided the heat keeps up to what is necessary, according to the season. To dry the inside of the frame in December, January, and February, let the linings be four or five inches above the level of the surface of the bed, which will be sufficient. In March and April they may be lowered in proportion to the increased power of the sun's heat. It may appear unnecessary to some persons to have the linings turned so often; but on the lively heat emanating from them the well-doing of the plants depends, especially when the heat of the bed begins to decline; and in proportion as attention is bestowed on them will be the success of the cultivator. If they are allowed to be undisturbed until they heat themselves dry, they become useless; and the same effect is produced if they get overcharged with moisture. In both cases, if not rendered entirely useless, they will take so long a time to recover their heat as to render them next to valueless; for where a warmth is requisite, in addition to that of the bed, the plants may be lost in the interval between the turning and re-rising of the heat. During the operation of turning, should there appear any part too much decayed, let it be removed, and its place filled with fresh linings, which should be put on the top of the old, in order to draw up the heat from it, and to keep up a good warmth round the frame; besides, when the new linings are above the bed there will be no danger of their rank steam getting to the plants. When the linings are again turned, the fresh manure applied must continue at the top; and, if necessary, some more must be added to it, in order that the right height may be preserved. It must, however, be observed, that the new linings should never be allowed to mix with the old ones until they have become quite sweet; for you must on no account allow rancied heat to be confined at the bottom of your linings. Attention to these directions must be continued until June, if it is desired to keep the plants in a healthy state; and although after the month of March the turnings need not be quite so frequent, a good warmth must be kept up, or the plants will not swell off their fruit kindly. Indeed, at an advanced period of the season, the roots will have got down into the dung; and as soon as that ceases to heat, they will perish from excess of moisture. (*Mills' Treat. on Cucumber*, 33.)

As the spring advances the glasses may be often taken off during mild days, or even to admit a light temperate rain. In June or July, according to the geniality of the season, they may be removed finally from beds and pits; and even before, the frames may be raised on bricks, so as to allow the runners to spread at will.

As it is important to keep up the temperature by linings, so must the unhealthy reduction of temperature within the frame at night be prevented by coverings placed over the glass. By preventing cooling, the necessity for increased heating is removed. The best mode of covering is to spread a little hay over the glasses; and to keep this in its place, as well as to exclude all wet, to place over it a coverlid of the asphalte cloth, which costs only a penny per square foot, and will last for years.

Mr. Duncan says that coverings of sugar-mats are the best; being thick, they do not lie close upon the glass, and being bad conductors prevent the radiation of heat from below; they are of a small size, and may be easily put on and removed; or, in milder weather, the spare lights of other frames may be used with advantage, particularly if the wind should be cold in the day. Cover the last thing at night, and uncover the first thing in the morning, under circumstances of a usual nature; but in extreme cases, such as frost, &c., of course it is done sooner and continued to a longer time, but never longer than eight or half-past eight o'clock. Mr. Duncan covers the middle of the glass only, lapping the mats over each other if necessary, but not else: a single one, merely covering the centre of the light, he says, is frequently all that is necessary; but when extremely cold, cover the whole glass. (*Culture of Cucumber*, 57.)

*Watering.* Water is usually required two or three times a week; it must be warmed as before mentioned previously to its application. Instead of watering the inside of the frame, it is a good plan to do so plentifully round the sides, which causes a steam to rise, and affords a moisture much more genial to the plants than watering the soil.

The quantity necessarily varies according to the circumstances of temperature and season. In wet, dull and cloudy weather, much less moisture is required by the plants than in bright sunshiny days. A common three-light frame, in good health and full bearing, will require eight gallons of water five evenings out of seven in very hot weather, such as we experienced in July; but sometimes, in dull weather, this quantity will serve them a week. (*United Gard. Journ.* 1846. 599.)

Mr. Mills, in his excellent "Treatise on the Culture of the Cucumber," says, watering frequently, and in small quantities, is the proper way to keep the plants in a sound state; but in the winter months, from the moisture of the fermenting material, and the absence of solar heat, they will require but little from the water-pot. The surface of the bed, near the frame, will occasionally become dry from the heat of the linings passing upwards through it; and when that occurs, let it be sprinkled with water, through a fine-rosed pot, just before covering up; and on fine mornings, about ten o'clock, give to the soil in which the plants are growing a little water in a tepid state. In November, December, and January, little water will be wanted, but in February, March, and April, more may be given; always, however, in the morning, and only when there is a prospect of the plants becoming dry by covering-up time. It is a bad practice to water late in the afternoon, even in April, May, and June, as the confined air, during the night, causes the damp to settle on the blossom of the fruit, when it destroys the pollen; and fruit so injured will seldom swell freely. If the soil within the frame be moderately moist, it will be sufficient for the night without late waterings. Where a doubt is entertained on this point, give a little to the sides of the frame, and not to the plants. In dull weather never water the plants, but the earth only.

*Impregnation.* Of late years it has been denied that impregnation is necessary for the production of fruit. That it is absolutely required, where seed is to be obtained, no one disputes. Mr. W. P. Ayres says, that so far as the production of fruit is concerned, impregnation is " neither good nor harm," and cites, in proof of this, a brace of fruit, which he cut on the 8th of February, 1840, each nineteen inches long, which had never been impregnated; for, at the time the female flowers were expanded, there was not a male blossom on the premises, and consequently no impregnation could take place.

Since that time, he has cut hundreds of fruit, the flowers of which never expanded, and the same has been done by several of his acquaintances. In fact, Mr. Wilson, Mr. Spivey, Mr. Judd, and the Messrs. Ayres, will undertake to procure, at the May *fete* of the Horticultural Society, from ten to twenty brace of fruit, as good as can be obtained by impregnation, the flowers of which shall be removed from the fruit before there is any chance of their being impregnated.

Where long fruit is desired, Mr. Ayres thinks, impregnation is positively injurious, because, if seed is the result of impregnation, the energy of the plant will be expended in perfecting the seed, instead of in the production of fruit, as every practical man knows that the production of one seed from it will weaken the plant more than a dozen of fruit fit for table. There are instances in nature, of plants perfecting their fruit without impregnation, as in the different varieties of figs; and why not the cucumber do the same? (*Gard. Chron.*, 1842. 172.)

Another practical gardener, Mr. Kyle, says, some years ago, as he was pegging down some plants, he broke the flower off the fruit, at least four or five days before it would have expanded. He left it, however, and, to his agreeable surprise, it swelled off as handsome a fruit as any he had during that season.

From that time he has never taken the least trouble respecting impregnation, unless when wanting to save seed. (*Ibid*. 1842. 237.)

Mr. W. Charlton gives similar testimony, for he says, some of the finest fruit he ever grew never opened a blossom. In one instance, he broke off the unexpanded corolla, and the end of the fruit, notwithstanding which, the fruit swelled, and was eaten at table. (*Ibid*. 253.)

Such testimony as this is unimpeachable as far as it can possibly be carried; which is no more than this, cucumbers unimpregnated have been known to attain a good size and perfection. But it by no means refutes the opinion, that, to be most certain of a fruit not falling immaturely, one condition is that it should be impregnated. To secure impregnation, as soon as a female blossom, which is known by having fruit beneath the flower-cup, opens, or on the second morning at farthest, a fresh full expanded male flower is to be plucked, with its footstalk pertaining to it, and the corolla or flower-cup being removed, the remaining central part or anther applied to the stigma of the female, which is similarly situated, and the fecundating dust discharged by gently twirling it between the finger and thumb. Fresh male blossom should be employed for every impregnation, and the operation performed in the early part of the day. An attention to this is only requisite to such plants as are in frames; those grown in the open air are always sufficiently impregnated by bees and other insects. When the male flowers appear in clusters they may be thinned moderately; but it is almost needless to deprecate the erroneous practice sometimes recommended of plucking them off entirely.

*For the production of seed,* some fruit must be left of the earliest forced production, as this is found to vegetate and produce fruit in much less time than that raised under hand-glasses, from whence the seed for the open-ground crops is usually obtained. The fruit that is left to produce seed should grow near the root, and upon the main stem, not more than one being left on a plant. They must remain as long as the seed can obtain any nourishment from the plant, which it does whilst the footstalk remains green; when this withers, and the rind of the cucumber has attained its full yellow hue, they may be gathered and reared in the sun until they begin to decay. The seed then being scraped out into a vessel, allowed to remain for eight or ten days, and frequently stirred, until the pulp attached to it is decayed, may be cleansed by frequent agitation in water; the refuse rises to the top, and passes away with the supernatant liquid. Being thoroughly dried by exposure to the air for three or four days, it is then fit for storing.

On this point, Mr. Duncan justly observes, that the finest specimens should be chosen to seed; those only which manifest a disposition to lengthen rapidly, and throughout alike and simultaneously; for those fruits which grow first by the footstalk seldom seed, and those at the apex seldom fail. When the fecundation of the stigma, by impregnation, takes place freely, the seed in embryo enlarges directly, consequently the fruit; and if the living principal becomes diffused generally into a great number of seed, it will grow equal; if less generally diffused, at the apex most, and *vice versa*. They should always be allowed to become well-ripened previous to being cut, and the seed never extracted until the latest desirable period before sowing. (*Duncan's Cult. of Cucumber*, 86.)

## DISEASES.

*Mildew*. There are many species of parasitical fungi, of which the mycelium, or spawn, pervades all nature, and is only waiting for the occurrence of favourable circumstances to vegetate and afflict the plants which are their peculiar pasturage. An atmosphere too moist, and a temperature somewhat too depressed, for the healthful vegetation of the plants on which those fungi prey, are contingencies especially favourable to the advance of these microscopic ravagers. This is a wise provision, for it is only the distempered juices of plants which are their food. No one ever saw the mildew upon the leaves of a healthy vigorous cucumber plant. So soon as it does appear, it is a signal for the gardener to increase the temperature, and diminish the moisture of the air in which the plants are growing, but to keep the roots duly supplied with water, and even a little liquid manure will do good. The juices of the plant have become too watery, and its vegetating energy diminished, therefore, let the free admission of light be facilitated by cleaning the glass, and accommodating the angle at which the frame is placed, so as to admit the greatest amount of solar rays. Remove any leaves that are most diseased, especially if others, by the removal, are exposed more freely to the light; dust the whole with flour of sulphur, sprinkle caustic slaked lime over the surface of the bed, and water, once a-week, moderately, with a solution of common salt, 2 ozs. to the gallon.

The Rev. M. J. Berkeley informs me, that the species of fungi most commonly occurring on the cucumber, are *Nichothecium roseum* (which really is a species of *Dactylium*), *Oidium erysiphoides*, and *O. leuconium*, both of which, Mr. Berkeley believes to be species of the genus *Erysiphe*.

*Barrenness* arises from the absence of female flowers when the plants do not produce fruit, and from the absence of pollen if fruit but not seeds are borne. Upon these defects the following observations from the pen of Dr. Lindley afford very satisfactory information. The late Mr. A. Knight, who was never guilty of forming an opinion upon any other than what he considered conclusive evidence, used to maintain that when plants have the stamens in one flower, and the pistil in another, it is possible to compel such plants to yield one or the other of such flowers at the pleasure of the operator. He found, in fact, by experiment, that the effect upon such plants of a preternaturally high temperature, was to cause them to produce male flowers only; while a preternaturally low temperature was favourable to the production of female flowers only. A water-melon plant was grown in a house, the heat of which was sometimes raised to 110 deg. during the middle of warm and bright days, and which generally varied in such days from 90 to 105 deg., declining during the evening to about 80 deg., and to 70 deg. in the night; the air was kept damp by copious sprinkling with water of nearly the temperature of the external air, and little ventilation was allowed. The plant under these circumstances grew with great health and luxuriance, and afforded a most abundant blossom, but all its flowers were male. This result, he says, did not in any degree surprise him; for he had many years previously succeeded, by long continued very low temperature, in making cucumber plants produce female flowers only; and he entertained little doubt that the same fruit-stalks might be made, in this and the preceding species, to support either male or female flowers,

" in obedience to external causes." This singular circumstance is explicable upon Morphological principles, and does not seem to be touched by any others. When the cucumber plant is ready to blossom, a part of the nascent leaves of some of the buds destined to become flowers will, under ordinary circumstances, form pollen in their cells, and become anthers, the central body being then destroyed by the operation ; while in other buds whose leaves form no pollen in their cells, the organising power is directed to the development of the central body, which then becomes a young fruit, bearing the rudiments of seeds. In that case which is the common and natural state of things each kind of flower assumes its habitual condition. But let the balance of organising forces lose its equipoise, so arrange things, that of the powers which mould the foliage while in its plastic condition, some one or other shall acquire an undue preponderance, as is most especially likely to happen to plants growing in an artificial climate, and the usual structure of the flower will be interfered with. It would seem that in the order of cucurbits, or at least in some of them, the power to form pollen in the cells of the plastic leaves is increased by heat ; and, that being so, to raise the temperature unduly, will have the effect of forming male flowers instead of females ; on the contrary, cold seems to interfere with the formation of pollen, and in that case a low temperature must produce females in preference to males. In what precise way a high temperature acts upon the cucumber, we cannot judge. We see the effects, but we cannot perceive the immediate operation of the cause. It is, however, notorious that there is something at work in nature which does influence the fashioning of leaves into stamens or carpels; and there is reason to believe that the former are often the result of increased vigour. Thus, in the hemp plant, the males may be known from the females by their larger size, and greater strength; and Fir trees will bear cones in the feebleness of youth, but not their clusters of stamens, till the tree is in the prime of its age. And it may very well be, that in the case of the cucumber the application of unwonted heat may have, and probably does have, the effect of so increasing the vital force, as to throw into the nascent leaves of the flower buds that quality which results in the development within their cells of the highly organised material called pollen. (*Gard. Chron.* 1845. 415)

*Canker*, like the spot in pelargoniums, is a peculiar ulceration, and having these characters. The plants usually grow very freely for some time, without any perceptible disease, or at the worst, looking rather yellow. By the time that any fruit is set, the leaves become spotted, the spots increase in number and size; the mid-ribs of the leaves are often nearly or quite severed in two wherever the disease touches;

next, the leafstalks, and then the vine itself, together with the fruit, suffer ; on a shoot, a foot in length, eight or ten small specks will often appear, looking as if some corrosive acid had been dropped on the parts in small quantities. These gradually spread. The occasion of the disease appears to be some sudden check to the supply of sap, after the plants have been brought to a high state of vigour and enlarged development of foliage. A decline in the temperature, or deficiency in the supply of water, render that development of foliage unnecessary, and from that moment its decay commences. I have known the canker at once banished by an increase of temperature, and an additional supply of water. It has been recommended, also, to impregnate the air of the frame with the fumes of sulphur, but I have no faith in applications of this, or any kind, to the parts diseased. Where the fumes of sulphur have been supposed to be beneficial, the benefit probably arose from the increased heat employed to obtain the fumigation.

*Gumming* is an exudation of gummy matter, which sometimes rises through the skin of the fruit. It appears to be an instance of extravasated sap arising from its being in excess, and will probably disappear by diminishing the supply of water slightly.

*Bitterness* is an ill quality of the fruit that may be removed by an increase of temperature and a freer exposure to the light. It arises from the imperfect elaboration of the juices; those in the neck of the cucumber, being least digested, are always more bitter than in any other part of the fruit.

*Deformity* of the fruit arises commonly from want of equable elaboration of the sap in all its parts. A crooked cucumber is usually most pale on the exterior side of the curvature, evincing that this side was least exposed to the light. A similar defect is produced by sudden changes of temperature; whether of that in which the foliage or the root is vegetating. Deformity particularly prevails if the plants be freely watered in dull or cold weather; it also often occurs when a few cold or wet days succeed very warm ones in the early part of the summer, and the heat of the bed has become exhausted; not unfrequently the bad effects may be observed for some time after the check, or rather the chill, has happened. Keeping plants warm and vigorous, and from sudden checks, is the best preventive; but insufficient light or water, and improper soil, cause deformity in the early part of the year. (*Ibid.* 1842. 97.)

---

## INSECTS.

*Green Fly* (Aphis cucumeris) very rarely appears, and never, I think, unless the plants have been very ill-cultivated. Syringing with tobacco-water destroys it.

*Thrips.* To kill these, syringe with tobacco-water, mixing that with a little sulphur, or a decoction of elder leaves. This, repeated a few times, will suffice. Another method is, to dust the infected parts with the flowers of sulphur, and in three or four days to wash it off with a syringe.

*Red Spider* (Acarus tellarius) will never appear if the soil and air have been kept properly moist. If it attacks the plants, fumigate them with sulphur, and increase the moisture.

# CONTENTS.

--------

## THE GOOSEBERRY.

# THE GOOSEBERRY.

---

## HISTORY.

THE gooseberry is especially a British fruit; for although, probably, it is not a native of these islands, yet it is now found wild in our hedge-rows; and in no other country is so much attention paid to its cultivation.

Although a native of Piedmont and other regions of northern Italy, yet, in its wild state, its fruit being small, acid, and flavourless, it does not appear to have attracted the care of the Roman cultivators, nor of any of our early continental ancestors; and it is not until the very commencement of the 16th century that we find it noticed in this country. Gesner thought the gooseberry is the *achanthakeanthos* of Theophrastus, but upon no satisfactory grounds. Dodoens, on whose botanical work our Lyte and Gerarde founded theirs, mentions the smooth-fruited gooseberry as the *Uva crispa;* Bauhine calls it *Grossularia sylvestris;* and Tusser, in his " Five hundred Points of Good Husbandry," published during

1557, mentions " gooseberries" among our then garden fruits.

Lyte, in 1578, says, " it is planted commonly almost along the borders of every garden." The green gooseberry he calls *Uva crispa;* and the *Uva ursi* of Galen, and *Ribes,* are names he applies to " the red-beyond-sea gooseberry;" but this is evidently our red currant, as his black gooseberry is our black currant.

Gerarde, in his " Herball," published 1597, says it is called *Fea-berry* in Cheshire. It has the same name in Lancashire and Yorkshire. This, in Norfolk, is abbreviated into *Feabes,* or, as the provincials pronounce it, *Fapes.* Gerarde says there were then " divers sorts, some greater, others less, some round, others long, and some of a red colour, growing in our London gardens and elsewhere in great abundance."

In the " Paradisus" of Parkinson, published in 1629, are described five varieties of gooseberries or feaberries : three reds, differing only in size ; one blue or purple, like the damson ; and one green and hairy, of which " the seed hath produced bushes bearing berries having few or no hairs upon them."

Johnson, in his edition of Gerarde (1636), has " the long green, the great yellowish, the blue, the great round red, the long red, and the prickly gooseberry." Ray has no English name but the pearl gooseberry. Rea mentions three sorts of the red, the blue, the yellow of several sorts, the White Holland, and the green, in his " Flora, Ceres, and Pomona," published during 1665. Miller only says, there were in his time (1724) several varieties obtained from seeds, most of them named from the persons who raised them, as Lamb's, Hunt's, Edwards's Gooseberry, &c.; but new ones being continually obtained, he considered it needless to enumerate them. (*Martyn's Miller's Dict.*)

In 1752 the attention of gardeners to raising improved varieties first becomes apparent; for Switzer, in his " Practical Fruit Gardener," then published, says, " the best sorts are the large white Dutch, the large amber, the early red and green, both hairy, Mr. Lowe's early green and walnut gooseberries, with some other very extraordinary kinds of his raising at Battersea, not yet named." Though this shews a somewhat awakened attention, yet the cultivation was still neglected; for Switzer, instead of pruning with the knife, recommends the bushes to be " clipt a little before Midsummer."

Hitt, in his " Treatise on Fruit Trees," is the first author who recommends a careful cultivation of this fruit " of the meaner sort," and gives directions for its pruning and general treatment.

Mr. Loudon observes, that the gooseberry is cultivated in greater perfection in Lancashire than in any other part of Britain; and next to Lancashire, the climate and treatment of the Lothians seem to suit this fruit. In Spain and Italy the fruit is scarcely known. In France it is neglected, and little esteemed. In some parts of Germany and Holland the moderate temperature and humidity of climate seems to suit the fruit; but in no country is its size and beauty to be compared with that produced in Lancashire, or from the Lancashire varieties cultivated with care in the more temperate and humid districts of Britain. Dr. Neill observes, that when foreigners witness our Lancashire gooseberries, they are ready to consider them as forming quite a different kind of fruit. Happily this wholesome and useful berry is to be found in almost every cottage garden in Britain; and it ought to be considered a part of every gardener's duty to encourage the introduction of its most useful varieties in these humble inclosures. In Lancashire, and some parts of the adjoining counties, almost every cottager who has a garden cultivates the gooseberry with a view to prizes gizen at what are called " gooseberry prize meetings ;" of these there is annually published an account, with the names and weight of the successful sorts, in what is called the *Manchester Gooseberry Book.* The prizes vary from 10s. to £5 or £10; the second, third, even to the sixth and tenth degrees of merit, receiving often proportionate prizes. There are meetings held in spring to " make up," as the term is, the sorts, the persons, and the conditions of exhibition ; and in August, to weigh and taste the fruit, and determine the prizes. In the " Gooseberry Book" is also announced annually the new-named seedlings which have been distinguished at former meetings and that are now " going out," that is, are about to be sold to the propagators. (*Enc. of Garden.* 732.)

It is in Lancashire, as just observed in the quotation from Loudon, and especially at Manchester, that gooseberry culture is carried to the highest degree of perfection. Mr. J. Clarkson, a resident in that vicinity, says that by consulting the gooseberry growers and their records, he found that 50 years ago the heaviest berries seldom exceeded 10 dwts. It was about that time that people began to cultivate the gooseberry in and about Manchester, being stimulated either by a spirit of emulation, or the value of the prizes. The perfection they attained owes nothing to men of scientific knowledge, being cultivated scarcely by any but the lowest and most illiterate members of society, but these, by continual experience and perseverance in growing and raising new sorts, have brought the fruit from weighing 10 to upwards of 30 dwts., and that, too, under the greatest disadvantages, not having the privilege of soil, manure, situation, &c., like the gardeners of their more wealthy neighbours, but oftentimes limited to a few yards of land, either shaded by trees, confined by buildings, or exposed to the most unfavourable winds, and so barren that they have frequently to carry on their shoulders a considerable way the soil in which the plants are to be set, yet so resolute are they in overcoming every obstacle, and so successfully ingenious in assisting nature in her efforts, that they are enabled to produce fruit surprisingly large. The oldest growers, some of them upwards of eighty years of age, were unable to tell Mr. Clarkson the time when, or the place where, the improvement of the gooseberry first commenced. Lists of several meetings which took place in 1786, are in existence in which the fruit is divided into four classes, red, yellow, green, and white, each class containing four sorts, making sixteen sorts at one meeting, no one sort being allowed to win more than one prize at the same show. The classification of the fruit, the number of meetings held at different places, and the variety of sorts .cultivated at the above time, sufficiently prove that meetings must have been held for exhibiting the fruit several years before.

The attention of the growers was early directed to the raising of new sorts, being encouraged by the liberal price given for each deemed to be a large one, all other properties being esteemed of secondary consideration ; so that we are now furnished with an extensive variety, possessing excellent qualities, both for size, quantity, beauty, and flavour. At present there is considerable latitude given at prize shows, as to the properties of this excellent fruit, some sorts being remarkable for their large size, such as the Roaring Lion, and Eagle; others, again, are remarkable for their beauty, such as the Lancashire Lad, Top Sawyer, Rockwood, Sovereign, Bonny Lass, and others; a third group are remarkable for their rich flavour, and a fourth for producing large crops; some sorts have their fruit large very early, while others are small until nearly ripe; some, again, bear large berries, but only a few of them, while other sorts bear both large and numerous berries; some sorts are ripe early, as Top Sawyer, Huntsman, and Rockwood, whilst others continue to grow much longer before they are ripe, such as the Printer, Duckwing, and several more. (*Gard. Mag.* iv. 483.)

---

## BOTANICAL CHARACTERS.

Dr. Martyn considers the name of goose-berry was applied to this fruit, in consequence of its being employed as sauce for that bird. It is somewhat unfortunate for this derivation that it never has been so used. It seems to me most probably to be a corruption of the Dutch name *Kruisbes*, or *Gruisbes*.

Kruisbes, I believe, was derived from Kruis, the Cross, and Bes, as Berry, because the fruit was ready for use just after the Festival of the Invention of the Holy Cross; just as Kruis-haring, in Dutch, is a herring, caught after the same festival. (*Sewel's Dutch Dict.*)

Its earliest botanical names were *Grossularia*, and *Uva crispa*; Linnæus being the first to unite it with the currant, under the generic title of *Ribes*.

*Ribes*, the gooseberry, is included in the Pentandria Monogynia class and order of Linnæus, and in the Natural order, *Grossulaceæ*. There are many sub-species, but not differing essentially from the following specific characters.

*Ribes Grossularia*, rough gooseberry. *Prickles*, solitary, or three together. *Branches*, spreading. *Footstalks*, hairy. *Stalks*, single flowered, with a two-leaved bractea. *Fruit*, hairy. *Shrub*, bushy, armed with awl-shaped prickles, in the place of stipulas. *Leaves*, bluntly three-lobed, and cut, slightly downy. *Flowers*, drooping, solitary, green, on downy stalks. *Calyx*, cup-shaped. *Germen* and *Fruit*, rough, with prominent bristly hairs. *Berries*, green, yellow, or red.

*R. Uva crispa*, smooth gooseberry, seems to be only a variety of the preceding.

## CHEMICAL COMPOSITION.

Green gooseberries have been analyzed by Mr.

Gerard, who examined the berries both before they were ripe, and when ripe. The constituents found in the two states were the following :—

|  | UNRIPE. | RIPE. |
|---|---|---|
| Chlorophylle (green colouring matter) | 0·03 | — |
| Sugar . . . . | 0·52 | 6·24 |
| Gum . . . | 1·36 | 0·78 |
| Albumen . . | 1·07 | 0·86 |
| Malic Acid . . . | 1·80 | 2·41 |
| Citric Acid . . | 0·12 | 0·31 |
| Lime . . . | 0·24 | 0·29 |
| Fibrin (including the seed) . | 8·45 | 8·01 |
| Water . . . | 86·41 | 81·10 |
|  | 100·00 | 100·00 |

*(Thomson's Vegetable Chem., 892.)*

The foregoing analyses show, that the acid constituents of gooseberries increase during ripening, though their presence is concealed by the simultaneous increase of the saccharine matter. The quantity of acid is further increased by exposure to a high temperature, and hence the reason that half-ripe gooseberries require more sugar to render them palateable than do unripe gooseberries, when employed in tarts. Instead of chlorophyle there is a peculiar red colouring matter in the red gooseberry.

## VARIETIES.

THE varieties of this fruit have now become very numerous, in proof of which, the list which follows is sufficient testimony. The information that list contains is principally derived from the "London Horticultural Society's Catalogue of Fruits."

*Duration.*—A gooseberry bush will live for many years under proper management, but it is never so vigorous for the production of fruit as from its fifth to its eighth year.

*Size.*—It must be always remembered that neither the amateur nor even the professed gardener will be able in most instances to grow berries equalling the size of those which they attained under the care of their original raisers. The particular treatment, probably, will not be adopted, and this is so well known among the growers for prizes that they avoid purchasing seedlings of their raisers until other growers have reported upon them.

*Selections.*—The following is a list of good flavoured and very large sized, those of each colour being placed in the order of ripening :—*Reds :* Keens's Seedling, Mellings's Crown Bob, Leigh's Rifleman, Boardman's British Crown, Red Warrington. *Whites :* Taylor's Bright Venus, Wellington's Glory, Saunder's Cheshire Lass, Woodward's Whitesmith, Cook's White Eagle. *Greens :* Parkinson's Laurel, Large Smooth Green, Collier's Jolly Angler, Massey's Heart of Oak, Edwards' Jolly Tar. *Yellows :* Didon's Golden Yellow, Prophet's Regulator, Prophet's Rockwood, Brotherton's Golden Sovereign, and Pilot.

The following are small, but of very good flavour. *Reds :* Red Champagne, Red Turkey, Rough Red, Ironmonger and Rob Roy. *Whites :* White Champagne, White Crystal, Early White, Taylor's Bright Venus and White Honey. *Greens :* Early Green Hairy, Pitmeston Greengage and Green Walnut. *Yellows :* Yellow Champagne and Rumbullion.

*For Bottling,* the best variety is the Rumbullion.

*For Preserving,* the best are the Red Champagne and the White Eagle. The first gives a deep red to the syrup, but the latter imparts as good a flavour and requires less sugar. Its syrup, made with loaf sugar, is slightly pink.

*Aaron* (Lovart's). Yellow, hairy, oblong, large. Second quality. Branches spreading.

*Abraham Newland* (Jackson's). White, hairy, oblong, large. First quality. Branches erect, excellent.

*Admirable* (Grange's).

*Ajax* (Gerrard's). Red, smooth, roundish, large. Third quality. Branches spreading.

*Alexander.* Red, hairy, obovate, large. Second quality. Branches spreading.

*Amber* (Amber Yellow, Smooth Amber). Yellow, smooth, roundish, small. Second quality. Branches spreading. Good bearer.

*Amber Hairy.* See Yellow Champagne.

*Ambush* (Cranshaw's.) White, smooth, obovate, large. Second quality. Branches erect. Late.

*Angler.* Green. Greatest weight 20 dwts. 1 gr.

*Anson's* (Colonel). Green, hairy, oblong, large. Third quality. Branches spreading. Late.

*Aston.* See Red Warrington.

*Aston Red.* See Red Walnut. Excellent.

*Aston* (Hebburn Yellow). Yellow, hairy, roundish, small. First quality. Branches erect.

*Aston Seedling.* See Red Warrington.

*Atlas* (Brundrett's. Brundretts Atlas). Red, hairy, oblong, large. Second quality. Branches erect.

*Audley Lass* (Williams'). Green, hairy, oval, large. Third quality. Branches spreading.

*Ball* (Yellow). Yellow, smooth, roundish. First quality. Branches erect.

*Balmure.*

*Bang-up* (Tyrer's). Red, hairy, roundish oblong, large. Third quality. Branches pendulous. Greatest weight 20 dwts. 12 grs.

*Bank of England* (Walker's). Dark red, smooth, obovate, large. Second quality. Branches pendulous. Pulp tinged with yellow.

*Battle of the Nile.* Red. Greatest weight, 18 dwts. 5 grs.

*Beauty of England* (Hamlet's). Red, hairy, oblong, large. Second quality. Branches spreading.

*Beauty* (Holt's). Green, downy, oblong, large. Second quality. Branches pendulous.

*Belmont.* Yellow. Greatest weight 13 dwts. 16 grs.

*Belmont's Green.* See Green Walnut.

*Bellingham.* Green. Greatest weight 14 dwts. 8 grs.

*Bell's Gift.* Green. Weight 24 dwts. 23 grs.

*Birdlime.* Yellow. Greatest weight 25 dwts. 15 grs.

*Billy Dean* (Shaw's). Red, smooth, obovate, large. Third quality. Branches spreading.

*Black* (Waverham's Bullfinch). Dark red, downy, obovate. Second quality. Branches spreading.

*Black Prince* (Shipley's). Dark red, downy,

roundish, middle size. Third qnality. Branches pendulous.

*Blithfield.* Yellow, smooth, round, small. Second quality. Branches erect. Late.

*Blucher.* Red. Greatest weight 17 dwts. 1 gr.

*Bloucher.* Green. Greatest weight 14 dwts. 21 grs.

*Boggart* (Houghtons). Dark red, smooth, obovate, very large. Third quality. Branches pendulous.

*Bonny Landlady* (Noble Landlady). White, hairy, oblong, large. Second quality. Branches erect.

*Bonny Lass* (Capper's). White, hairy, oblong, large. Second quality. Branches spreading. Berry handsome. Greatest weight 21 dwts. 10 grs.

*Bonny Roger* (Diggles's). Yellow, smooth, obovate, large. Second quality. Branches spreading. Greatest weight 20 dwts. 10 grs.

*Bottom Sawyer* (Capper's). Yellow, downy, obovate, large. Second quality. Branches spreading. Leaves downy above.

*Bright Venus* (Taylor's). White, hairy, obovate, middle size. First quality; branches erect; excellent. Hangs till it shrivels.

*Britannia* (Sister's). Yellow, downy, obovate, large. Third quality. Branches spreading.

*British Crown* (Boardman's). Red, hairy, roundish, very large. Second quality. Branches spreading. Greatest weight 20 dwts. 20 grs.

*British Hero.* Red. Greatest weight 17 dwts. 10 grs.

*British King.* Green. Greatest weight 12 dwts. 5 grs.

*British Prince* (Boardman's). See Boardman's Prince Regent.

*Brownsmith.*

*Bullfinch.* See Waverham's Black.

*Bumper.* Green. Good bearer. Greatest weight 24 dwts. 16 grs.

*Bunker's Hill* (Capper's). Yellow, smooth, round-ish, large. Second quality. Branches spreading.

*Burdett.* Red. Greatest weight 16 dwts. 19 grs.

*Captain Greenall.* Green. Greatest weight 13 dwts. 17 grs.

*Captain* (Red). *Captain* (White).

*Catharina.* Yellow. Greatest weight (1845) 30 dwts. 4 grs.

*Chadwich.* White. Greatest weight 15 dwts. 19 grs.

*Chain.* Yellow. Greatest weight 18 dwts. 20 grs.

*Champagne* (Green). Green, smooth, roundish, small. Third quality. Branches erect. Leaves downy above.

*Champagne* (Barclay's green). Green, smooth, roundish, middle size. Third quality. Branches spreading.

*Champagne* (Large Pale). Green, downy, round-ish, oblong, small. First quality. Branches pendulous. Leaves downy.

*Champagne* (Red). Red Turkey (of some); Dr. Davis' Upright; Countess of Errol; Ironmonger (of many). Red hairy, roundish, oblong, small, First quality. Of unequalled richness. Pulp clear. Branches remarkably erect.

*Champagne* (White). White, hairy, roundish, oblong, small. First quality. Branches erect. Leaves pubescent.

*Champagne* (Yellow. Hairy Amber). Yellow, hairy, roundish, small. First qulaity. Branches erect. Excellent.

*Chance* (Green). Green, downy, oblong, large. Third quality. Branches pendulous.

*Charles Fox* (Monck's). Green, hairy, ovate, small. Second quality. Branches erect.

*Cheshire Lady.* Red, hairy, oblong, middle size. First quality. Branches erect. Late. Excellent.

*Cheshire Cheese* (Hopley's), Yellow, smooth, oblong, large. Third quality. Branches spreading. Greatest Weight 17 dwts. 8 grs.

*Cheshire Lass* (Saunder's). White, downy, oblong, large. First quality. Branches erect. Earliest and best to gather green for tarts. Greatest weight, 19 dwts. 1 gr.

*Chisel.* Pale green, smooth, oblong, large. Third quality. Branches spreading. Skin thin.

*Chisel.* Green. See Viner's Green Balsam.

*Chorister.* White. Greatest weight, 12 dwts. 19 grs.

*. Chrystal.* White, smooth, roundish, small. First quality. Branches spreading. Late. Good bearer.

*Chrystal.* (Red).

*Chrystal* (White). White, hairy, downy, roundish, small. First quality. Branches spreading.

*Claret.* Red, smooth, roundish, small. Second quality. Branches spreading.

*Colonel Holding.* Yellow. Greatest weight, 17 dwts.

*Commander.* Red. Greatest weight, 16 dwts.

*Companion.* Red. Very large. Greatest weight, 31 dwts. 5 grs.

*Competition.* White. Greatest weight, 22 dwts. 1 gr.

*Conquering Hero* (Chipendale's). Green, hairy, oblong, middle size. Third quality. Branches spreading. Bad bearer.

*Conquering Hero* (Catlow's). Green, yellow, hairy, oblong, middle size. Third quality. Branches erect.

*Conquering Hero.* Red. Greatest weight (1845), 30 dwts. 18 grs.

*Conqueror* (Fisher's. Cook's Defiance). Greenish yellow, smooth, oblong, large. Third quality. Branches spreading. Bad bearer. Greatest weight, 16 dwts. 12 grs.

*Conqueror* (William's). Red, hairy, obovate, large. Second quality. Branches pendulous.

*Conqueror* (Worthinton's). Red, smooth, obovate, large. Third quality. Branches pendulous. Late.

*Cornwall.* Dark, hairy, oblong, large. Third quality. Branches pendulous.

*Corduroy.* Green. Greatest weigh, 15 dwts. 8 grs.

*Cossack.* White. Greatest weight (1845), 25 dwts. 16 grs.

*Cotgrave.* Red. Greatest weight, 17 dwts.

*Cottage-girl* (Heap's). Greenish yellow, hairy, oblong, large. Third quality. Branches erect.

*Counsellor Brougham.* Green, white, downy, oblong, large. Second quality. Branches spreading. Good bearer.

*Countess of Errol.* See Red Champagne.

*Creedus.* Yellow. Greatest weight 14 dwts. 2 grs.

*Creeping Ceres.* Yellow. Greatest weight, 14 dwts. 12 grs.

*Crown Bob* (Melling's). Milling's Crown Bob. Red, hairy, oblong, large. First quality. Branches spreading. Very good. Considered most profitable and therefore most cultivated by Lancashire Market Gardeners. Preserves well. Greatest weight 22 dwts. 17 grs.

*Croyer's Favourite.* Green. Greatest weight, 15 dwts. 10 grs.

*Croyer's Red.* Red. Greatest weight, 15 dwts. 10 grs.

*Dakin's Black.* Dark red, downy, oblong, middle size. Second quality. Branches erect. Bad bearer.

*Damson* (White). White, smooth, roundish, small. First quality. Branches erect. Skin thin.

*Dark Red* (Large.)

*Dr. Davis's Upright.* See Red Champagne.

*Defiance* (Cook's). See Fisher's Conqueror.

*Defiance* (Worthinton's). Red, hairy, obovate, large. Second quality. Branches pendulous. Greatest weight, 28 dwts.

*Delight* (Weedham's). Needham's Delight. Green, yellow, hairy, oblong, large. Third quality. Branches pendulous. Bad bearer. Greatest weight, 19 dwts. 8 grs.

*Double-bearing* (Eckersley's). See Red Walnut.

*Downy Yellow.*

*Drap d'Or.*

*Dublin.* Yellow. Greatest weight (1845), 26 dwts. 16 grs.

*Duchess.* White. Greatest weight, 14 dwts. 6 grs.

*Duck Wing* (Buerdsill's). Yellow, smooth, obovate, large. Second quality. Branches erect. Late.

*Dudley and Ward.* Pale red, smooth, oblong, large. Third quality. Branches pendulous.

*Duke of Waterloo.* Yellow. Greatest weight, 16 dwts. 11 grs.

*Duke of York* (Allcock's). See Leigh's Rifleman.

*Dumpling.* See Scotch best Jam.

*Dusty Miller* (Stringer's). Greenish white, smooth, obovate, middle size. Second quality. Branches pendulous. Greatest weight 14 dwts. 10 grs.

*Earl of Denbigh.* Green. Greatest weight, 14 dwts. 22 grs.

*Earl Grosvenor.* Red, downy, obovate, large. Second quality. Branches pendulous. Greatest weight 21 dwts. 9 grs.

*Earl Moira.* Red. Greatest weight, 17 dwts. 2 grs.

*Early Black.* Dark red, hairy, oblong, middle size. Second quality. Branches pendulous.

*Early green Hairy.* Early Green. Green Gascoigne. Green, hairy, round, small. First quality. Branches spreading. Early and good.

*Early Rough Red.* Red, hairy, roundish, oblong. Second quality. Branches spreading.

*Early Red.*

*Early White.* White, downy, roundish, middle size. First quality. Branches spreading.

*Elijah* (Lovart's). Red, hairy, roundish, large. Second quality.

*Elisha* (Lovart's). Green, hairy, roundish, large. Second quality. Branches spreading. Greatest weight, 18 dwts. 21 grs.

*Emperor Napoleon* (Rival's). Red, smooth, obovate, large. Second quality. Branches, pendulous. Good bearer. Late. Greatest weight, 22 dwts. 18 grs.

*English Rose.* Red. Greatest weight, 17 dwts. 16 grs.

*Evergreen* (Perring's). Green, smooth, oblong, large. Third quality. Branches spreading. Greatest weight, 18 dwts. 12 grs.

*Expectation.* Green. Greatest weight, 14 dwts. 23 grs.

*Fair Play.* Green. Greatest weight, 14 dwts. 16 grs.

*Fair Rosamond.* White. Greatest weight, 15 dwts. 12 grs.

*Fame.* Green, smooth, obovate, large. Third quality. Branches pendulous.

*Farmer.* See Chapman's Jolly Farmer.

*Farmer's glory* (Berry's). Red, downy, obovate, large. First quality. Branches pendulous. Good bearer.

*Favourite* (Bates'). Green, smooth, oblong, middle size. Second quality. Branches pendulous. Greatest weight, 19 dwts. 4 grs.

*Favourite* (Smith's). Red, hairy, roundish oblong, middle size. Second quality. Branches spreading.

*Fig* (White). White, smooth, obovate, small.

First quality. Branches spreading. Rich; but a tender plant.

*First Rate* (Parkinson's). White, smooth, oval, large. Second quality. Branches pendulous. Greatest weight, 21 dwts.

*Fleur de Lis.* White. Early. First quality.

*Fowler* (Grundy's). White, downy, obovate, middle size. Third quality. Branches spreading. Greatest weight, 17 dwts. 8 grs.

*Foxhunter.* Red. Greatest weight (1823), 25 dwts. 2 grs.

*Freedom.* White. Greatest weight (1845), 27 dwts. 8 grs.

*Friend Ned.* Red. Greatest weight, 16 dwts. 2 grs.

*Fudler* (Leigh's). White, smooth, oblong, middle size. Third quality. Branches pendulous. Greatest weight, 14 dwts. 22 grs.

*Gallant.* Green. Greatest weight, 15 dwts. 2 grs.

*Gascoigne green.* See Early Green Hairy.

*Gascoigne* (White.)

*George the Fourth.* See Red Champagne.

*Gibraltar.* Greenish yellow, smooth, oblong, middle size. Third quality. Branches pendulous. Greatest weight, 14 dwts. 15 grs.

*Gingler.* Green. Greatest weight, 14 dwts. 9 grs.

*Glasgow Youth.* Red. Greatest weight, 15 dwts. 1 grs.

*Glenton green.* York Seedling. Green, hairy, oblong, middle size. First quality. Branches pendulous. Very good. Leaves pubescent.

*Globe* (Green). Green, hairy, round, small. Second quality. Branches spreading. Coarse.

*Globe* (Hopley's). Yellow, hairy, round, large. Third quality. Branches pendulous. Greatest weight 20 dwts.

*Globe* (Large Red). Red, hairy, roundish, large. Second quality. Branches erect.

*Globe* (Small Red). Smooth Scotch, Red, smooth, roundish, small. First quality. Branches erect. Sharp rich flavour.

*Globe* (Yellow).

*Globe Yellow* (of some). See Rumbullion.

*Globe of Europe.* White. Greatest weight 11 dwts. 12 grs.

*Glorious* (Bell's). Speechly's Highwayman. Red, hairy. Greatest weight (1817) 26 dwts. 17 grs.

*Glory of England.* Yellow, downy, obovate, large. Third quality. Branches pendulous.

*Glory of Kingston.* Green, smooth, roundish, middle size. Third quality. Branches spreading. Bad bearer.

*Glory of Oldham.* Red, hairy, oblong, middle size. Second quality. Branches spreading.

*Glory of Ratcliff* (Allen's). Green, smooth, oblong, middle size. First quality. Branches spreading.

*Glory* (Whitton's). Dark red, smooth, oblong, middle size. Second quality. Branches pendulous.

*Golden Ball.* See Early Sulphur.

*Ditto Bess.*

*Ditto Bull.* See Early Sulphur.

*Ditto Chain* (Forbes's). Yellow, smooth, oblong, large. Third quality. Branches pendulous.

*Golden Drop.* Golden Lemon. Yellow, downy, roundish, middle size. Second quality. Branches erect. Greatest weight 11 dwts. 18 grs.

*Golden Eagle* (Nixon's). Yellow, downy, roundish, small. Second quality.

*Golden Fleece* (Part's). Yellow, hairy, oval, large. First quality. Branches pendulous. Resembles Golden Drop.

*Golden gourd* (Hill's). Green, yellow, hairy, oblong, large. Second quality. Branches pendulous.

*Golden Lemon.* See Golden Drop.

*Golden Orange* (Jackson's). Bright yellow, hairy, oblong, large. Third quality. Branches pendulous.

*Golden Purse* (Bamford's). Barnfort's Golden Purse. Yellow, smooth, obovate, large. Third quality. Branches pendulous.

*Golden Queen* (Kay's). Lay's Golden Queen. Greenish yellow, smooth, roundish, large. Third quality. Branches pendulous.

*Golden Sovereign* (Bratherton's). Yellow, hairy, roundish, large. Second quality. Branches spreading.

*Golden Yellow* (Dixon's). Greenish yellow, smooth, turbinate, middle size. Second quality. Branches pendulous.

*Goliath Champion* (Costerdine's). Greenish yellow, smooth, oblong, large. Second quality. Branches pendulous.

*Goliath* (Rider's). Yellow, smooth, obovate, middle size. Third quality. Branches erect.

*Gourd.* Yellow. Greatest weight 18 dwts. 1 gr.

*Governess* (Bratherton's). Green, white, hairy, roundish oblong, large. Second quality. Branches spreading.

*Governor* (Bratherton's).

*Great Britain.* Greenish white, smooth, oblong, large. Second quality. Branches pendulous. Greatest weight 15 dwts. 18 grs.

*Great Captain* (Hooper's). Red, smooth, oblong. large. Second quality. Branches spreading.

*Great Chance.* See Farrow's Roaring Lion.

*Great Tup. Green Anchor* (Bell's). Coarse.

*Green Balsam* (Viner's). Green Chisel. Green, smooth, obovate, large. Third quality. Branches pendulous. Greatest weight 16 dwts. 2 grs.

*Green Bob.* Green. Greatest weight 13 dwts. 19 grs.

*Green Drop.* Green. Greatest weight 12 dwts. 11 grs.

*Greenfield Joan.* Yellow. Greatest weight 15 dwts.

*Green-gage* (Horsefield's). Green, smooth, roundish, large. Third quality. Branches spreading. Greatest weight 12 dwts. 4 grs.

*Green-gage* (Pitmaston). Green mottled with red, smooth, obovate, rather small. First quality. Branches erect. Prickles few. Excellent; very sugary, and will hang till it becomes shrivelled.

*Green-globe.* Green, round, middle size. Second quality. Branches spreading.

*Green Isle.* Green. Greatest weight 13 dwts. 5 grs.

*Green Knight.* Green. Greatest weight 14 dwts. 12 grs.

*Green Mountain* (Sandiford's). Green, hairy, oval, large. Third quality. Branches spreading.

*Green Myrtle* (Nixon's). Green, smooth, oblong, large. Second quality. Branches pendulous.

*Green Oak.* Green, hairy, roundish, large. Second quality. Branches erect.

*Green Ocean* (Wainman's). Ingham's Green Ocean. Green, smooth, oblong, large. Third quality. Branches pendulous.

*Green Page.* Green. Greatest weight 12 dwts. 6 grs.

*Green Prolific* (Hebburn's). See Hebburn's Green Prolific.

*Green Rock.* Green. Greatest weight 12 dwts. 9 grs.

*Green Seedling.* Green, hairy, oblong, small. First quality. Branches pendulous. Good bearer.

*Greensmith.* Green, hairy, roundish, middle size. Second quality. Branches erect.

*Green Willow.* Green, downy, roundish, large.

Third quality. Branches erect. **Bad bearer.** Greatest weight 19 dwts. 20 grs.

*Green Willow.* See Parkinson's Laurel.

*Greenwood* (Berry's). Pale green, smooth, oblong, large. Second quality. Branches pendulous. Good bearer. Greatest weight 18 dwts. 8 grs.

*Gunner.* Yellow. Greatest weight 23 dwts. 20 grs. Bears well. Second quality.

*Haddingtonshire.* White. Greatest weight 11 dwts. 2 grs.

*Hairy Black.* See Ironmonger.

*Hairy green* (Gerrard's). Green, hairy, roundish, middle size. Third quality.

*Hairy Red* (Barton's). Red, hairy, roundish, small. Second quality. Branches erect. Good bearer.

*Hall's Seedling.* See Woodward's Whitesmith.

*Hawk.* Yellow. Greatest weight 21 dwts. 8 grs.

*Haywood's Defiance.* Red. Greatest weight 15 dwts. 19 grs.

*Heart of Oak* (Massey's) Green, smooth, oblong, large. First quality. Branches pendulous. Good bearer. Greatest weight 17 dwts. 6 grs.

*Hebburn green Prolific.* Green, hairy, roundish, middle size. First quality. Branches erect. Excellent.

*Hedgehog.* See Irish White Raspberry.

*Hero* (Ambersley). Dark, red, smooth, oblong, large. Third quality. Branches spreading.

*Hero* (Kilton). See Hamlet's Kilton.

*Highlander* (Horsfield's). Yellow, downy, oblong, large. Third quality. Branches erect. Bad. Greatest weight 16 dwts. 3 grs.

*High Sheriff of Lancashire* (Grundy's). Green, smooth, obovate, middle size. Second quality. Branches pendulous.

*Highwayman* (Speechley's). See Glorious Bell.

*Hit or Miss* (Taylor's). Red, hairy, oblong, very large. Third quality. Branches pendulous. Coarse.

*Honey* (White). White, smooth, round, oblong, middle size. First quality. Branches erect. Excellent.

*Hogg's Seedling.* Green. Greatest weight 12 dwts. 1 gr.

*Huntsman* (Bratherton's). Speechley's Rough Robin. Dark red, hairy, roundish, large. Second quality. Branches erect. Great bearer. Greatest weight (1820) 25 dwts. 18 grs.

*Husbandman* (Foster's). Forester's Husbandman. Yellow, downy, obovate, large. Second quality. Branches erect.

*Incomparable.* White. Greatest weight 16 dwts. 7 grs.

*Independent* (Brigg's). Bigg's Independent. Green, smooth, obovate, large. Second quality. Branches erect. Good bearer. Greatest weight 18 dwts. 17 grs.

*Invincible* (Heywood's). Yellow, downy, round, oblong, large. Second quality. Branches erect. Greatest weight 17 dwts. 22 grs.

*Invincible.* Green. Greatest weight 25 dwts. 5 grs.

*Irish Plum.* Dark red, hairy, roundish, middle size. First quality. Branches erect.

*Ironmonger.* Hairy Black. Red, hairy, roundish, small. First quality. Branches spreading. Leaves pubescent; fruit more round and darker than that of red Champagne; a superior variety often confused with this.

*Ironmonger.* See Red Champagne.

*Jackson's Slim.* Dark red, downy, obovate, middle size. Second quality. Branches spreading.

*Jagg's Red.* Red, smooth, roundish, large. Second quality. Branches pendulous.

*Jay Wing.*

*John Bull* (Blomerley's). Yellow, downy, obovate, large. Second quality. Branches pendulous.

*Joke* (Hodkinson's). Green, downy, roundish. large. Third quality. Branches pendulous.

*Jolly Angler* (Colliers's). Collin's Jolly Angler. Lay's Jolly Angler. Green, downy, oblong, large. First quality. Branches erect. A good late sort. Greatest weight 17 dwts.

*Jolly Cobler.* Green. Greatest weight 13 dwts. 21 grs.

*Jolly Farmer* (Chapman's). Prince of Wales. Farmer. Green, smooth, oblong, large. Third quality. Branches spreading; greatest weight 17 dwts. 13 grs.

*Jolly Gunner* (Hardcastle's). Royal Gunner. Yellow, hairy, oblong, large. Third quality. Branches erect.

*Jolly Miner* (Greenhaigh's). Red, smooth, obovate, large. Third quality. Branches pendulous. Greatest weight 21 dwts. 14 grs.

*Jolly Nailor* (Bromley's). Greenish white, hairy, roundish, oblong, large. Third quality. Branches erect. Greatest weight 16 dwts. 11 grs.

*Jolly Printer* (Eckersley's). Eckersley's Jolly Painter. Dark red, smooth, oblong, large. Third quality. Branches spreading.

*Jolly Tar* (Edward's). Green, smooth, obovate, large. First quality. Branches pendulous. Good bearer. Greatest weight 16 dwts. 14 grs.

*Juniper.* Green. Greatest weight 15 dwts. 19 grs.

*Jubilee* (Hopley's). Dark red, hairy, roundish, large. Second quality. Branches erect. Greatest weight 22 dwts. 17 grs.

*Keens's Seedling.* Keens's Seedling Warrington. Very dark red, hairy, oblong, middle size. First quality. Branches pendulous. Good bearer; earlier than red Warrington; grows dwarf.

128

*Kilton* (Hamlet's). Kilton Hero. Greenish yellow, hairy, oblong, large. Second quality. Branches pendulous. Greatest weight 15 dwts. 5 grs.

*King* (Allcock's). Dark red, hairy, roundish, large. Second quality. Branches erect; greatest weight 15 dwts. 21 grs.

*Lady Delamere* (Wild's). Yellow, white, smooth, oblong, large. Third quality. Branches spreading.

*Lady Lilford* (Grundy's). See Woodward's Whitesmith.

*Lady of the Manor* (Hopley's). White, hairy, roundish oblong, large. Second quality, Branches erect. Greatest weight, 20 dwts. 2 grs.

*Lancashire Hero.* Red. Greatest weight, 17 dwts. 6 grs.

*Lancashire Lad* (Hartshorn's). Dark red, hairy, roundish, large. Second quality. Branches erect. Good bearer. Fruit very handsome. Greatest weight, 21 dwts. 14 grs.

*Lancashire Lass.* See Woodward's Whitesmith.

*Langley green* (Mills'). Pale green, hairy, roundish, large. Second quality. Branches erect. Greatest weight, 16 dwts. 15 grs.

*LargeEarlyWhite.* Greenish white, downy, obovate, large. First quality. Branches erect. Very Early.

*Large White.* White, downy, oval, middle size. Second quality. Branches pendulous. Early.

*Large Yellow.* Greenish yellow, smooth, obovate, middle size. Branches pendulous.

*Late green.* Green, downy, obovate, small. First quality. Branches erect.

*Laurel* (Parkinson's). Green Laurel, Green Willow (of some). Pale green, downy, obovate, large. First quality. Branches erect; good bearer; nearly a white, resembling Woodward's Whitesmith. Greatest weight 19 dwts. 1 gr.

*Leader.* Yellow. Greatest weight 28 dwts. 14 grs.

*Lion* (White). White, hairy, obovate, large. Third quality. Branches erect.

*Lioness* (Fennyhaugh's). White, smooth, obovate, large. Second quality. Branches pendulous.

*Little John.* Dark red, hairy, oblong, small. Second quality. Branches erect.

*Little Red Hairy.* See Rough Red.

*Lively Green* (Boardman's). Like Parkinson's Laurel. Greatest weight, 18 dwts. 5 grs.

*London.* Red. Largest known. Greatest weight (1841), 35 dwts. 12 grs. This was grown by Mr. T. Gibson, of Nottingham, and was considered " The Champion Berry of England," but, in 1845, Mr. Elliot, of Ounsdale, grew one, weighing 36 dwts. 16 grs.

*Long Yellow.* Green, yellow, smooth, oblong, large. Second quality. Branches spreading.

*Lord Combermere.* (Forester's). Yellow, smooth, obovate, large. Second quality. Branches spreading.

*Lord Crew* (Hopley's). Green, hairy, oblong, large. First quality. Branches erect. Greatest weight, 23 dwts.

*Lord Hood* (Tartlow's). Pale, green, smooth, obovate, large, third quality. Branches erect. Greatest weight, 12 dwts. 21 grs.

*Lord of the Manor* (Bratherton's). Red, hairy, roundish, large. First quality. Branches spreading.

*Lord Suffield* (Haywood's). Green, yellow, smooth, obovate, large. Third quality. Branches pendulous.

*Lord Wellington* (Howley's). Red, smooth, oblong, large. Branches spreading.

*Lord Valentia.* White, smooth, oblong, large. Third quality. Branches spreading.

*Lovely Anne.* Green, downy, oval, large. Second quality. Branches pendulous.

*Magistrate* (Diggle's). Red, downy, obovate, large. First quality. Branches spreading.

*Magnum Bonum.* Red. Greatest weight, 16 dwts. 14 grs.

*Maid of the Mill* (Stringer's). White, downy, obovate, middle size. First quality. Branches erect. Greatest weight, 15 dwts. 17 grs.

*Major.* Green. Greatest weight, 14 dwts. 14 grs.

*Major Cartwright.* Red. Greatest weight, 18 dwts. 19 grs.

*Marchioness of Devonshire.* White. Greatest weight, 17 dwts.

*Marchioness of Downshire.* White, hairy, oblong, middle size. Third quality. Branches erect.

*Marquis of Granby.* White. Greatest weight, 15 dwts. 1 gr.

*Marquis of Stafford* (Knight's). Red, hairy, round, oblong, large. Second quality. Branches spreading. Resembles Wilmot's Late Superb.

*Matchless* (Wright's). Dark red, hairy, oblong, middle size. Third quality. Branches pendulous.

*Meager.* Yellow. Greatest weight, 16 dwts. 17 grs.

*Medal.* Yellow. Greatest weight, 16 dwts. 9 grs.

*Mermaid.* White. Greatest weight, 15 dwts. 14 grs.

*Merry Lass.* Green, smooth, obovate, middle size. Second quality. Branches erect. Greatest weight, 16 dwts. 20 grs.

*Merryman* (Nuts). Pale green, downy, obovate, middle size. Second quality. Branches pendulous. Greatest weight, 17 dwts. 4 grs.

*Midsummer.* Green, smooth, roundish, small, second quality. Branches erect. Early.

*Mignonette.* Green, hairy, roundish, small. Second quality. Branches erect. Leaves pubescent.

*Milkmaid.* White. Greatest weight, 17 dwts. 9 grs.

*Minerva.* Green, smooth, oblong, large. Third quality. Branches spreading.

*Miss Bold.* Pigeon's Egg (of some). Red, downy, roundish, middle size. First quality. Branches spreading. Early. Allied to Red Walnut, but better.

*Miss Hammond.* White. Good bearer. Greatest weight, 24 dwts. 6 grs.

*Miss Walton.* White. Greatest weight (1845), 24 dwts. 19 grs.

*Mogul.* Red. Greatest weight, 20 dwts. 15 grs.

*Moses* (Lovart's). Green, hairy, obovate, large. Second quality. Branches erect.

*Moss's Seedling.* See Early Sulphur.

*Moston Pile.* White. Greatest weight, 15 dwts. 10 grs.

*Mountaineer.* Green. Greatest weight, 12 dwts. 9 grs.

*Mrs. Clark.* Green. Greatest weight, 16 dwts. 12 grs.

*Murrey.* See Red Walnut.

*Napoleon* (Saunder's). Yellow, smooth, obovate, large. Second quality. Branches pendulous.

*Nelson.* Green. Greatest weight, 14 dwts. 21 grs.

*Nelson's Waves* (Andrew's). Yellowish green, hairy, oblong, large. Third quality. Branches pendulous. Greatest weight, 22 dwts. 8 grs.

*Noble Landlady.* See Bonny Landlady. Greatest weight, 16 dwts. 22 grs.

*No Bribery* (Taylor's). Green, smooth, obovate, large. Second quality. Branches pendulous.

*Nonpareil.* See Green Walnut.

*Nonsuch.* Red. Greatest weight, 18 dwts. 12 grs.

*Northern Hew.* Green, smooth, obovate, large.

Third quality. Branches pendulous. Greatest weight, 14 dwts. 3 grs.

*Nutmeg.*

*Ditto* (of some). See Raspberry.

*Nutmeg* (Brawnlie). Red, smooth, obovate, small. Second quality. Branches spreading.

*Nutmeg* (Scotch). Red, hairy, downy, roundish. Second quality. Branches erect.

*Old Ball.*

*Old England* (Rider's). Dark red, smooth, round, oblong, large. Second quality. Branches pendulous. Resembles Wilmot's Early red.

*Old Preserver.* See Raspberry.

*Old Scotch Red.* See Rough Red.

*Ostrich.* White. Greatest weight, 24 dwts. 3 grs.

*Overall.* Green. Greatest weight, (1845) 25 dwts. 7 grs. Good bearer.

*Ditto* (Bratherton's). Red, hairy, oblong, large, second quality; branches pendulous; greatest weight, 22 dwts.

*Pastime* (Bratherton's). Dark red, hairy, roundish, large, second quality; branches pendulous; extra bracts often attached to the sides of the fruit; greatest weight, 20 dwts. 14 grs.

*Patriot.* Red. Greatest weight, 20 dwts. 2 grs.

*Peacock.* Green; greatest weight (1845), 26 dwts. 5 grs.; flavour resembling greengage plum; not a good bearer.

*Peover's-pecker*, Bell's. Dark green, smooth, obovate, large, third quality; branches pendulous; greatest weight, 19 dwts. 10 grs.

*Perfection*, Gregory's. Green, downy, roundish, large, first quality; branches, pendulous; late.

*Phantom.* Green; greatest weight, 14 dwts. 9 grs.

*Philip the First.* White; good bearer; greatest weight, 24 dwts.

*Pigeon's Egg* (of some). White, hairy, obovate, middle size.

*Ditto.* See Miss Bold.

*Pilot.* Yellow; greatest weight, 27 dwts. 5 grs.

*Platoff.* Green; greatest weight, 13 dwts. 22 grs.

*Platt's White.* Greenish white, hairy, roundish, small, first quality; branches, erect.

*Ploughboy,* Grundy's. Red; greatest weight, 16 dwts. 15 grs.

*Polander.* Red; greatest weight, 18 dwts. 22 grs.

*Pollet's Seedling.* Dark red, smooth, oblong, large. Third quality. Branches spreading.

*Prince of Orange* (Bell's). Yellow, downy, oblong, large. Second quality. Branches pendulous.

*Prince of Wales.* See Chapman's Jolly Farmer.

*Prince Regent* (Bordman's). Boardman's British Prince. Dark red, smooth, roundish, large. Second quality. Branches spreading. Greatest weight 24 dwts. 1 gr.

*Princess Royal.* Green, white, hairy, obovate, large. First quality. Branches pendulous. Good bearer.

*Printer.* Red. Greatest weight 20 dwts.

*Profit* (Prophet's). Green, downy, oblong, large. Second quality. Branches spreading.

*Providence.* Green. Greatest weight 21 dwts. 10 grs.

*Porcupine* (Henderson's). See Irish White Raspberry.

*Purse.* Yellow. Greatest weight 17 dwts. 7 grs.

*Queen.* Yellow. Greatest weight 18 dwts. 19 grs.

*Queen Ann* (Sampson's). Simpson's Queen Ann. Greenish white, downy, ovate, large. Second quality. Branches erect. Greatest weight 20 dwts. 6 grs.

*Queen Caroline* (Lovart's). White, smooth, obovate, middle size. Second quality. Branches erect.

*Queen Charlotte* (Peer's). Greenish white, hairy, oblong, middle size. First quality. Branches erect. Greatest weight 16 dwts. 12½ grs.

*Queen Mary* (Morris's). Greenish white, downy, ovate, middle size. Third quality. Branches erect. Greatest weight 15 dwts. 22 grs.

*Queen of Trumps.* White. Greatest weight, (1845), 24 dwts.

*Queen Victoria.* Green. Greatest weight, 1845, 26 dwts.

*Quoiter.* Yellow. Greatest weight 15 dwts 1 gr.

*Radical,* Smith's. White, hairy, roundish oblong, large, second quality; branches pendulous.

*Ranger.* Yellow, hairy, roundish, small, third quality; branches pendulous; greatest weight 17dwts 16 grs.

*Ranter.* White. Greatest weight 14 dwts 3 grs.

*Raspberry.* (Old Preserver. Nutmeg of some). Darkish red, hairy, roundish, small, first quality; branches spreading; early.

*Raspberry,* Irish White. Henderson's Porcupine, Hedgehog. White, hairy, roundish, small, first quality; branches spreading; fruit very hispid.

*Ratcliff.* Green. Greatest weight 17 dwts 15 grs.

*Ratcliff ringers.* Red. Greatest weight 19 dwts 20 grs.

*Rattlesnake.* Yellow. Greatest weight 13 dwts 21 grs.

*Red,* Beaumont's. Dark red, hairy, roundish, middle size, first quality; branches erect, leaves pubescent.

*Red Mogul.* Red, hairy, roundish, small, first quality; branches spreading.

*Red Ocean.* Red. Greatest weight 16 dwts 17 grs.

*Red Oval,* Large. Red, hairy, oval, large, first quality; branches spreading.

*Red Rose.* Red, downy, oblong, large, first quality ; branches pendulous ; very good.

*Red Smith.* Red, downy, oval, middle size ; second quality ; branches spreading.

*Red.* Thick-skinned. See Rough Red.

*Red Tukey.* Smooth Red. Red, smooth, obovate, small ; first quality ; branches spreading.

*Red Turkey* (of some). See Red Champagne.

*Reformer.* Green, smooth, oblong, large ; second quality ; branches spreading.

*Regulator* (Prophet's). Yellow, downy, roundish, large ; second quality ; branches pendulous.

*Richmond-hill* (Ward's). Dark red, smooth, obovate, large : second quality ; branches pendulous.

*Rifleman* (Leigh's). Allcock's Duke of York, Yates's Royal Ann, Grange's Admirable. Red, hairy, roundish, large ; first quality ; branches erect ; good bearer, late ; greatest weight 17 dwts. 5 grs.

*Ditto* (London). Green, smooth, oval, middle size ; third quality ; branches spreading.

*Ringleader* (Johnson's). Red, smooth, oblong, large ; second quality ; branches pendulous.

*Roaring Lion* (Farrow's). Great Chance. Red, smooth, oblong, very large ; second quality ; branches pendulous ; late, and one of the very largest ; greatest weight, 1825, 31 dwts. 16 grs.

*Robin Hood* (Bell's). Yellowish green, downy, oblong, large ; branches pendulous.

*Rob Roy.* Red, hairy, obovate, middle size ; first quality ; branches erect ; very early.

*Rockgetter.* White ; greatest weight 16 dwts. 2 grs.

*Rockwood* (Prophet's). An old sort. Yellow, hairy, roundish, large, second quality ; branches erect, early, bears well ; berry handsome ; greatest weight 21 dwts. 3 grs.

*Rodney* (Acherley's). Red, downy, obovate, middle size, second quality; branches pendulous; allied to Red Walnut.

*Rough red.* Little Red Hairy, Old Scotch Red, Thick-skinned Red. Red, hairy, roundish, small, first quality; branches spreading; esteemed for preserving.

*Ditto.* New.

*Ditto* (Small Dark). Small Rough Red. Red, hairy, round, small, first quality; branches spreading, early, leaves pubescent; very good for preserving.

*Rough Robin* (Speechley's) See Huntsman (Bratherton's).

*Ditto Yellow.* See Sulphur.

*Ditto White* (Early). White, hairy, oval, large, second quality; branches erect.

*Round Yellow.* See Rumbullion.

*Royal Ann* (Yates's). See Leigh's Rifleman.

*Ditto Duke.* Dark red, smooth, obovate, large, third quality; branches pendulous.

*Ditto George.* Green, smooth, oval, middle size, second quality; branches erect.

*Ditto,* Early. Green, hairy, oblong, middle size, second quality; branches pendulous.

*Ditto Gunner,* Hardcastle's. See Hardcastle's Jolly Gunner.

*Ditto Oak.* Red, hairy, roundish, middle size, first quality; branches spreading.

*Royal,* Pearson's. White, downy, oval, middle size, second quality; branches spreading.

*Ditto Rockgetter,* Saunder's. Andrew's Royal Rockgetter. White, downy, obovate, large, second quality; branches erect.

*Ditto white.* White, hairy, round, small, first quality; branches erect.

*Ruleall.* Yellow; greatest weight 16 dwts. 4 grs.

*Rumbullion.* Yellow Globe, Round Yellow. Pale yellow, downy, roundish, small, second quality;

branches erect; great bearer; much grown for bottling.

*Rumbullion*, Green. Green, hairy, round, small, second quality; branches erect.

*Sabine's green.* Green, smooth, roundish, small, first quality; branches spreading.

*Saint John.* Red, smooth, obovate, middle size, second quality; branches spreading.

*Samson.* Red; greatest weight 16 dwts. 1 gr.

*Scarlet*, Transparent. Dark red, hairy, roundish, small, second quality; branches erect; bad bearer.

*Scented Lemon*, Rider's. Red, smooth, obovate, large, first quality; branches spreading; very good.

*Scotch green*, Green; greatest weight 12 dwts.

*Scotch best Jam.* Dumpling. Dark red, hairy, roundish, small, first quality; branches erect, leaves pubescent.

*Scotch Lass.* Green; greatest weight 12 dwts 12 grs.

*Self-Interest.* Yellow; greatest weight 15 dwts 6 grs.

*Shakspeare*, Denny's. Red, hairy, roundish, large, first quality; branches erect.

*Shannon*, Hopley's. Green, smooth, roundish, large, third quality; branches spreading; greatest weight 15 dwts 18 grs.

*Sheba Queen*, Crompton's. Compton's Sheba Queen. White, downy, obovate, large, first quality; branches erect; ripens early, good bearer; extremely near, if not the same as Woodward's Whitesmith; greatest weight 18 dwts 14 grs.

*Shepherd.* Yellow; greatest weight 15 dwts 10 grs.

*Silversmith.* White; greatest weight 11 dwts 10 grs.

*Sir Francis Burdett*, Mellor's. Light red, hairy, obovate, large, second quality; branches erect.

*Sir John Cotgrave*, Bratherton's. Dark red, hairy,

obovate, large, third quality; branches pendulous; greatest weight 25 dwts 2 grs.

*Sir Sidney Smith.* See Woodward's Whitesmith.

*Small green.* Green, downy, globular, small, second quality; branches erect.

*Small hairy green.* Green, hairy, roundish, small, second quality; branches erect, leaves pubescent.

*Small red.* Red, hairy, roundish, small, first quality; branches spreading.

*Smiling beauty*, Beaumont's. Yellow, smooth, oblong, large, first quality; branches pendulous; good bearer, skin thin.

*Smiling girl*, Haslam's. White, smooth, roundish, oblong, large, second quality; branches erect.

*Smithy-ranger*, Fidler and Bullock's.

*Smolensko*, Greaves's. Red, smooth, oblong, large, second quality; branches pendulous; greatest weight 21 dwts 10 grs.

*Smooth Scotch.* See Small Red Globe.

*Ditto green.* See Green Walnut.

*Ditto*, Large. Green, smooth, obovate, large, first quality; branches spreading.

*Ditto red.* See Red Turkey.

*Ditto yellow.* Yellow, downy, roundish, small, first quality; branches erect.

*Smuggler*, Beardsell's. Yellow, smooth, roundish, oblong, large, third quality; branches spreading.

*Snowball*, Adam's. White, hairy, roundish, middle size, first quality; branches pendulous.

*Snowdrop.* White; greatest weight 11 dwts 12 grs.

*Sovereign.* Yellow; berry handsome; greatest weight 22 dwts 17 grs.

*Southwell Hero*, Smith's. Green; greatest weight 16 dwts 11 grs.

*Sparklet.* Greenish yellow, downy, obovate, small, second quality; branches pendulous.

*Speedwell*, Taylor's. Greenish white, hairy, oblong, large, second quality; branches pendulous.

*Sportsman*, Chadwick's. Dark red, smooth, obovate, large, second quality; branches spreading; greatest weight 20 dwts.

*Squire Hammond*, Lovart's. Red, hairy, roundish, large; greatest weight 23 dwts 20 grs.

*Statesman*, Billington's. Red; greatest weight 22 dwts.

*Striped Green.*

*Striped Yellow.*

*Sugar-loaf.* White; greatest weight 12 dwts 19 grs.

*Sulphur.* Rough Yellow. Yellow, hairy, roundish, small, first quality; branches erect; leaves not pubescent; greatest weight 11 dwts 20 grs.

*Sulphur*, Early. Golden Ball, Golden Bull, Moss' Seedling. Yellow, hairy, roundish oblong, middle size, second quality; branches erect, very early, and a good bearer.

*Tallyho.* White. Good bearer; greatest weight, 1845, 25 dwts 14 grs.

*Tantararara*, Hampson's Red, downy, obovate, middle size, first quality; branches erect, leaves pubescent.

*Teazer.* Yellow. Greatest weight, 1830, 32 dwts 13 grs; good bearer, very beautiful, first quality.

*Thrasher*, Yates'. Greenish white, smooth, oblong, large, third quality; branches pendulous, greatest weight, 30 dwts. 12 grs.

*Thumper.* Green. Greatest weight 29 dwts 12 grs.

*Tim Bobbin*, Clegg's. Greenish yellow, smooth, oblong, middle size, second quality; branches erect; greatest weight, 17 dwts. 3 grs.

*Toper*, Leigh's. Fox's Toper. Greenish white, downy, oblong, large, third quality; branches pendulous; greatest weight, 18 dwts.

*Top Sawyer*, Capper's.   Pale red, hairy, roundish, large, second quality; branches pendulous, greatest weight, 1819, 26 dwts. 17 grs., berry handsome.

*Trafalgar*, Hallow's. Warwickshire Hero. Greenish yellow, hairy, oblong, large, third quality; branches pendulous, greatest weight 19 dwts. 13 grs.

*Tramp*.   Green, greatest weight 18 dwts. 12 grs.

*Transparent*.   White, greatest weight 14 dwts. 18 grs.

*Trimmer*.   Dark red, smooth, obovate, large, third quality; branches pendulous.

*Triumph*, Ryder's.   Green, hairy, obovate, small, third quality; branches spreading.

*Triumphant*, Denny's.   Red, hairy, obovate, large, second quality; branches pendulous, greatest weight 23 dwts. 4 grs.

*Troubler*, Moore's.   Green, hairy, roundish, oblong, large, second quality; branches spreading, greatest weight 15 dwts 16.

*Trueman*.   Greenish white, hairy, obovate, large, second quality; branches erect.

*Turnout*.   Green, greatest weight 23 dwts 14 grs.

*Two-to-one*.   Yellow, greatest weight, 1845, 28 dwts.

*Unicorn*.   Green, downy, oval, large, second quality; branches spreading.

*Union*.   Green, greatest weight 13 dwts 13 grs.

*Unknown*.   Green, greatest weight 13 dwts 21 grs.

*Victory*, Lomas's.   Red, hairy, roundish, large, second quality; branches pendulous, much esteemed for cooking.

*Victory*, Mather's. Yellow, smooth, obovate, large, second quality; branches spreading.

*Ville de Paris*, Gradwell's.   Greenish yellow, smooth, obovate, large, third quality; branches pendulous, greatest weight 17 dwts 17 grs.

*Viper*, Gorton's.   Green, yellow, smooth, obovate,

large, second quality; branches pendulous; greatest weight, 21 dwts. 2 grs.

*Vittoria*, Denny's. Greenish white, smooth, obovate, large, second quality; branches spreading; greatest weight, 17 dwts. 3 grs.

*Volunteer*. See Red Warrington.

*Walnut*, Green. Belmont's Green (of some), Smooth Green, Nonpareil. Dark green, smooth, obovate, middle size, first quality; branches spreading; great bearer.

*Walnut*, Red. Murrey, Eckersley's Double Bearing, Ashton Red (of some). Red, downy, obovate, middle size, second quality; branches spreading; early.

*Walnut*, White. Yellowish white, smooth, obovate, large, first quality; branches erect.

*Wanton*, Diggle's. Greenish white, smooth, roundish, middle size, second quality; branches spreading.

*Warrington*, Red. Aston, Aston Seedling, Volunteer. Red, hairy, roundish oblong, large, first quality; branches pendulous; one of the best late varieties; pulp clear.

*Warrior*, Knight's. Light red, downy, obovate, large, second quality; branches pendulous.

*Warwickshire Hero*. See Hallow's Trafalgar.

*Waterloo*, Sydney's. Green, downy, oblong, middle size, third quality; branches pendulous; greatest weight 13 dwts 6 grs.

*Weathercock*. Green; greatest weight (1845), 24 dwts 6 grs.

*Wellington*. Red; greatest weight, 16 dwts 6 grs.

*Wellington's Glory*. White, downy, roundish oblong, large, first quality; branches erect; skin thin and beautifully transparent; flavour excellent; tolerable bearer; greatest weight, 20 dwts.

*Whipper-in*, Bratherton's. Dark red, smooth, oblong, large ; second quality ; branches pendulous ; greatest weight, 26 dwts 16 grs.

*White Bear*, Moore's. White, hairy, obovate, large, first quality ; branches erect.

*White Eagle*, Cook's. White, smooth, obovate, large, first quality ; branches erect ; very late ; most beautiful of all the varieties ; bears well ; excellent for preserving ; greatest weight, 24 dwts. 9 grs.

*White Heart*, Nixon's. White, hairy, heart-shaped, middle size ; third quality ; branches erect.

*White Lily*. White, downy, obovate, middle size, second quality ; branches erect.

*White Lion*, Cleworth's. White, downy, obovate, large, first quality ; branches pendulous ; a good late sort.

*White Ocean*. White ; greatest weight, 15 dwts 7 grs.

*White Rock*. White ; greatest weight, 17 dwts 14 grs.

*White Rasp*. White, smooth, round, small, second quality ; branches spreading.

*White Rose*, Neill's.

*White Rock*, Brundrett's. Brundit's White Rock. White, smooth, obovate, large, third quality ; branches pendulous.

*Whitesmith*, Woodward's. Whitesmith, Sir Sydney Smith, Hall's Seedling, Lancashire Lass, Grundy's Lady Lilford. White, downy, round, oblong, large, first quality ; branches erect ; excellent flavour, and a good bearer ; greatest weight, 17 dwts 17 grs.

*Wilmot's Early Red*. Dark red, smooth, roundish oblong, large, second quality ; branches pendulous.

*Wilmot's Late Superb*. Red, hairy, roundish oblong, large, second quality ; branches spreading. Like Knight's Marquis of Stafford.

*Wilmot's Seedling Red*. Dark red, smooth, oblong, large, second quality ; branches spreading.

*Winter white.* White; greatest weight, 15 dwts 8 grs.

*Wistaston Green.* Green; greatest weight, 14 dwts 9 grs.

*Wistaston Hero,* Bratherton's. Green, hairy, oblong, large, second quality; branches erect; greatest weight, 15 dwts. 16 grs.

*Wistaston Lass.* White.

*Witherington.* Red; greatest weight, 14 dwts 5 grs.

*Wonderful.* Red; greatest weight (1845), 32 dwts.

*Woodman.* Red; greatest weight, 17 dwts 7 grs.

*Yaxley Hero,* Speechley's. Red, hairy, obovate, large, first quality; branches erect; greatest weight (1818), 24 dwts 14 grs.

*Yellow Beauty.* Yellow; greatest weight, 11 dwts. 12 grs.

*Yellow Hornet,* Williamson's. Williams's Yellow Hornet. Yellow, downy, obovate, small, second quality; branches erect.

*Yellow,* Kelk's. Yellow, downy, oblong, middle size, second quality; branches erect.

*Yellow,* Old Dark. Yellow, smooth, roundish, small, second quality; branches erect; leaves pubescent.

*Yellowsmith.* Yellow, hairy, roundish, oblong, small, first quality; branches erect; resembles Yellow Champagne.

*Yellow,* Waverham's. Yellow, downy, oval, middle size, second quality; branches pendulous.

*York Lass.* White; greatest weight 11 dwts.

*York Seedling.* See Glenton Green.

# STANDARD OF MERIT.

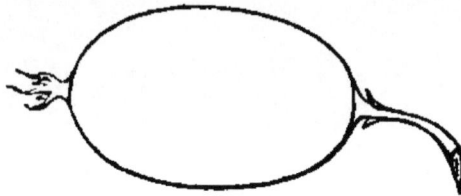

*Flavour.*   Rich and sugary.

*Size.*   Not less than 18 dwts.

*Form.*   If ovate, greatest diameter three-fifths of its extreme length; and if round, the nearest to a perfect globe.

*Nose (Calyx) and Stalk.*   On slight elevations of the berry.

*Skin.*   Very thin, yet not liable to burst.   In the hairy sorts, the hairs slight and regularly disposed.

*Colour.*   The purer the more desirable.   No red or yellow gooseberry has its beauty more diminished than by being veined with green.

The time has now arrived when the raiser of gooseberries should aim primarily at flavour, for nothing further is desirable in the increase of size.   If one gooseberry weighed 20 dwts., and another of 18 dwts. was equal to it in all other characteristics, but superior to it in flavour, I would award the prize to the latter.   No one can grow gooseberries weighing 18 dwts. without great care and skill; and this being secured, the most desirable objects, beyond controversy, are their palateableness and culinary utility.

## SOIL AND MANURES.

ALTHOUGH the gooseberry can be grown in almost any garden soil, yet, if excellence of fruit is desired, the soil must be a rich loam, not less than 12 inches deep, and resting on a well-drained yet cool subsoil. The plantation should be near the bottom, yet on the side, of a hill, and be unshadowed by trees, for if these intercept from them the light, the fruit will be neither large, nor full coloured, nor high flavoured. Whether to form an entirely new soil, or to improve that in which the plantation is to be made, the following compost, recommended by Mr. Haynes, may be advantageously adopted.

Of fresh or maiden earth from a light loamy rich pasture, take one whole spit-deep, with all the turf; to which add one-fourth of rotten stable litter, prefering that from an old hotbed made in the previous spring, which, from its softness and greater readiness to intermix with new soil, will be found preferable to every other; add one-fourth of the finest soft and black bog earth, or, in default of this, either the same quantity of the darkest coloured tree-soil (vegetable earth), prefering that from the more hard-wooded trees, as oak, ash, elm, or fruit-trees, or the same quantity of fully decayed tree-leaves; mix the whole regularly together, laying it in one narrow heap or ridge, about a yard high, in any situation exposed to the sun and air, there to remain six, nine, or twelve months, as circumstances may admit; turning over the whole every three weeks, the weather being favourable, that the entire heap may be thoroughly incorporated. The longer the compost remains in this state, the more advantageous it will prove. (*Haynes' Cult. of Gooseberry,* 79.)

This compost being formed early in the spring, and duly prepared by repeatedly turning over, will be in fit condition to apply when planting either in September or October. The gooseberry, like other trees, has its favourite or genial soil, and this is bog earth, applied in moderate quantity. It renders the soil open for the smallest fibres of this finely-rooted plant, and cool to promote increasing growth of the fruit during the summer months. Whoever has noticed the growth of the gooseberry in various soils and situations will have observed those growing on dry soils, however well cultivated, to have produced fruit of very inferior size, even when our summers have not been unusually warm. As a further proof that warmth, in conjunction with a dry soil, is unfavourable to the perfection of this fruit, it is well known that in the American State of New York, where the summers are more hot than in England, that the large fruited varieties taken from this country produce berries of such insignificant growth as not to merit culture; and the prize cultivators of this fruit in Lancashire prefer cool and rich soils. (*Ibid.*)

Mr. Levingston says that the soil should be trenched at least two spits deep, and strongly manured with composts or dung, according to the nature of the soil: if this be light, manure with cow-dung, pond mud, scourings of dishes, sprats, sea-ware, &c.; if the soil be cold and heavy, with stable-dung, pigeon-dung, soot, ashes, &c.; all of which are either to be used in composts or simple, but composts are to be prefered. If the new plantation ground be taken in from a pasture, it should be trenched full three spits deep, laying the top turf upside down, at the bottom of the trench. (*Growth of the Gooseberry,* 35.)

The soil for promoting the rooting and growth of cuttings should be prepared by removing the soil to the depth of three inches, and then putting in a layer of compost two inches thick, composed principally of decayed leaves, and on this an inch deep of the soil of the garden. In this bed the cuttings should remain two years, and instead of planting the trees in the common soil, and placing the manure over the roots, remove the soil to the depth of one foot or 18 inches, to be replaced either with Haynes' compost or a mixture of the soil of the garden, if good, with old stable manure, broken bones, and a considerable portion of decayed leaves.

*Manures.* These have already been noticed incidentally; and I have only to add, that in obtaining large gooseberries, *liquid manure*, formed of guano or pigeons' dung (and if of the guano, not more than half an ounce to each gallon of water), will be found very effective. Apply this in March, April and May. In the latter month it is a good plan to place mulch upon the surface over the roots of the trees; its fertilizing particles are washed down to them, and in dry weather it retains to them moisture. Soap-suds and the drainage from a dung-hill, in equal proportions, have also been employed beneficially as a liquid manure to the gooseberry.

## PROPAGATION.

*By Seed.* This is the mode for obtaining new varieties. The seed must be taken from perfectly ripe berries, dried by spreading on a sheet of blotting paper, and sown immediately in pots of light loam, to remain in the greenhouse during winter, or be preserved in sand until February, and then sown. If kept unsown and dry until the spring the seed often remains without germinating for 12 months. The soil must be kept moderately moist until the seedlings are large enough to prick out in beds, which will be in October, and this removal must be into a rich moist soil in a warm situation. Seedlings will bear when three years old. There is no doubt that improved varieties might be raised by skilful hybridizing, but I am not aware that it has been adopted, the raisers usually being satisfied with the chance impregnated seed from some favourite variety. The Red Champaigne, if impregnated with pollen from the London, I believe, would yield offspring bearing very superior fruit.

Mr Levingston, nurseryman, Parson's Green, Middlesex, gives these directions for the culture of seedlings : Make the bed four feet wide, alloting two spare feet between each bed for the alleys, and with a wooden headed, or cuffing, rake draw and push the back of the rake evenly from one side of the bed to the other, moving the surface about one or two inches deep, and laying it up in a ridge at the extremity of each side of the bed. Sow the seeds regularly between the two ridges, and smooth it with the back of the spade ; then with the front and back of the rake, draw back the surface earth regularly over the seeds, covering them about one inch deep, with the lightest and driest of the soil. The seedlings will soon appear above the surface, when they will require to be kept clear of weeds, and gently watered if dry hot weather. When they are about two inches in height thin them to about six or eight inches apart, and water when required until winter. *(Levingston on the Gooseberry)*.

The following year prune the seedlings to a clear

stem twelve or eighteen inches in height, leaving only three, four, or five buds or eyes at the top of the stem to form the head. If dry weather continues, they will require gently watering frequently, to facilitate their growth. Keep them clear from weeds, and go over them at different times in the course of the spring and summer, displacing any suckers arising from the roots, or laterals from the stems. The third year, as the gooseberry bears its fruit principally on young shoots of the previous summer's growth, that wood is now to be left entire as there will be a likelihood of the plants having some fruit on the ensuing season, and which may be depended upon as a true specimen of its future merits. But if it should happen that the season should be wet, or the bush not in a good state of health, it may not bear any fruit until the following year; or if not vigorous, and the season is unfavourable for ripening fruits, an imperfect berry may be produced; in which cases the bush is not to be condemned until it has had a more favourable chance of proving itself another year. *(Ibid)*.

*Layering* might be resorted to if the shoots are few in number and it is desirable not to risk the failure of a cutting; a risk, however, that is very trifling.

*Suckers* are rarely or never employed for propagating the gooseberry, because they have numerous adventitious buds low down towards the soil, from which, and perhaps from habit of growth, the plants thus raised are very liable to generate suckers. This is objectionable because the production of suckers robs the branches of sap which would have been devoted to their development and the production of fruit.

Mr. Levingston also deprecates raising plants from either layers or suckers, because, he says, by the first mode the bushes can hardly be obtained handsome, and by the second they are more liable to disease.

*Cuttings* are most usually employed for increasing desired varieties. The following are very good directions for their preparation. Shoots of the same year's production must be employed, and for the purpose, the best shoots are those that are fully ripened, robust, but not too strong. They are first to be deprived of about two or three inches of the point, and cut into lengths of ten inches or a foot, according to the size and strength of the shoots. Then, with a sharp knife, divest each shoot of the whole of its buds, excepting three or four nearest the top of the cutting, which must be left to form the branches of the future plant. Rubbing off the buds is not sufficient; they require to be picked out, or pared very close, to prevent them from throwing up suckers. The small buds towards the base of the cutting are always the most troublesome in this respect, and great care should be taken to remove them effectually before the cutting is inserted in the ground. Immediately underneath the part which the lowest bud occupied, make a clean horizontal cut without displacing any portion of the bark, and the cutting is then complete. Insert the cuttings in rows a foot apart, six or eight inches asunder, and two or three inches deep, pressing the earth firmly round them, either with the hand, or by placing one foot on each side of the row and treading it from one end to the other. (*Gard. Chron.* 1841. 732.)

The removal of the buds from the lower portion of the cutting should be done very effectually, and Mr. D. Cameron is quite right in his recommendation, that they should be cut clean out of the solid wood, much in the same way as a bud is taken off for inserting in a stock. A sharp knife, and a little experience, will enable the operator to make cuttings in this way as expeditiously as by the usual method, if only cutting the buds clean off without wounding the stem. At the base of the buds are sometimes left, by the usual method, the embryos of future buds, which in time become suckers. (*Ibid*, 102.)

*The emission of roots* from the cuttings is promoted in various ways, and the earlier this emission is produced the better, because the sooner and more effectually does the growth of the future shrub commence. This protrusion of roots is induced by removing, in the beginning of August, a ring of bark from the lower part of the shoots intended for cuttings ; a callus soon forms, and by applying wet moss or soil to the part, roots are readily emitted. In September, when nearly all the leaves are fallen, cut them from the trees and plant them; and, as soon as all the leaves have fallen, prune them back to the three or four buds which are intended to form the branches, and, of course, all buds below these must be carefully cut out. (*Ibid*. 1842. 84.)

If the above plan is not adopted, Mr. R. Lymburn, of Kilmarnock, states, that the cuttings (in winter) always succeed best when the articulation, or socket, that joins the young branch to the old, is pulled out along with the cutting, when separated from the bush. If thus extracted from the parent shrub, and planted in a situation shaded from the mid-day sun, these slips will root if planted in July and August. When planting, a small quantity of wet moss is tied on the bottom of the cutting, which induces roots to develop themselves abundantly, and thus a proportionate number of fine shoots are made. When the plants are taken up in the autumn, the moss is removed, and the bottom roots only are allowed to remain. (*Ibid*. 1841, 781.)

## GENERAL CULTURE.

*Planting.* The preparation of the soil has already been noticed in a previous section, therefore I have only to observe here upon the insertion of the shrubs. The gooseberry, like most other trees and shrubs, succeeds best with its roots growing near the surface. Shallow planting, therefore, has to be adopted ; and I quite assent to the following directions given by Mr. Levingston.

Plant the bushes in an upright manner, and not deeper than just to cover the top part of the roots, about two inches below the surface ; spread these out regularly and unentangled, taking care to shake the plant regularly as the earth is falling round the roots, that it may completely surround them, and place them in a sound, proper bed, giving them a gentle tread with your foot, and a little water to moisten the soil if it be dry. (*Levingston's Growth of the Gooseberry*, 36.)

The bushes are best planted in a quincunx order, thus—

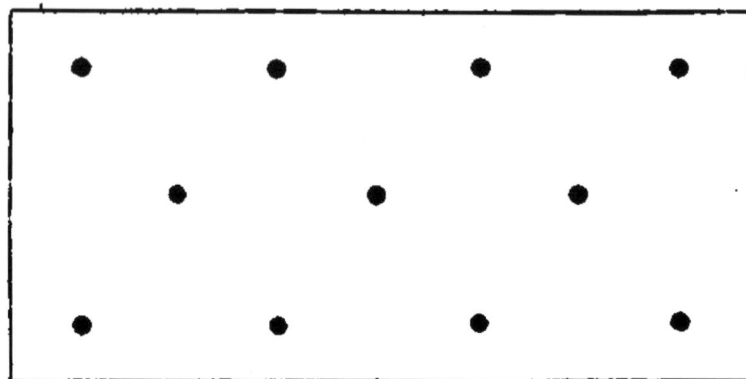

and the rows six feet apart, and at the same intervals in the rows.

*Pruning.* The pruning necessary for young plants has already been detailed, and our attention may now be confined to that which they require to promote their productiveness. It must always be borne in mind that the gooseberry bears almost exclusively, and always the finest fruit, upon the shoots produced the year previously.

All shoots which grow where they are not wanted should be cut clean out; and it should be borne in mind in pruning that it is the end buds which generally produce shoots, and consequently you may make a shoot grow in any direction you please by cutting the wood back to a bud which points in that direction. (*Gard. Chron.* 1842, 84.)

After these general directions, we may proceed to more particular details, of which the best have been furnished by Mr. Saul, one of the principal Lancashire gooseberry cultivators. He says—

As all the fruit grows from the underside of the branches, the plan adopted for first putting the tree in a training state, is to have a few hooked and forked sticks, the former to hold down the branches that are inclined to grow upwards, and the latter to support those which are inclined to grow downwards. The plant in the sketch on the next page has been trained by such sticks. It consists of three shoots spreading regularly, and nearly horizontally outwards. Next autumn these three shoots will have produced side shoots most of which may be shortened to one eye, and the

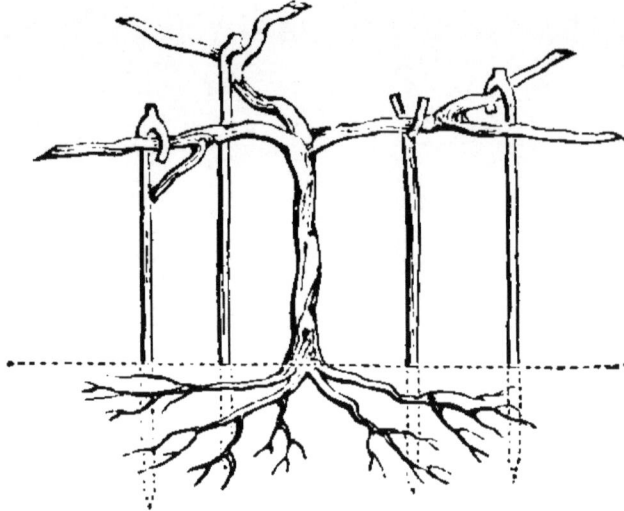

others reduced to one half of their length. No shoots should be left either at the origin or the extremities of the branches, but only at the sides; the fewer the number of shoots, and the younger the tree, the larger will be the fruit. At the next pruning season, viz. November, the tree will consist of the three principal shoots, each bearing two young shoots shortened to about 7in. of their length; these last, in the succeeding year's pruning, are to be left with two shoots only of new wood; all other shoots are to be closely cut out; and, in leaving the young shoots for bearing, regard must be had to keep the whole in a regular and handsome form. In all following years, the system of pruning and thinning is to keep a moderate and constant supply of strong healthy young shoots, from which alone can be expected large and fine fruit; and, when the extremities grow

beyond the proper bounds, such branches should be
cut back, so as to keep the tree in a compact form,
and furnished sufficiently, though rather thinly, with
new bearing wood : for large fruit cannot be expected
if the tree is too much crowded. *(Gard. Mag.* iii.
421).

*Espaliers.*—Gooseberries are highly improved by
being grown upon bushes trained as espaliers, which
may be planted along borders near the side walks of
the kitchen garden, but they are far better grown in a
separate compartment. For these the trellis must not
be higher than three feet from the ground, and for the
purpose stakes about four inches in circumference, and
thus arranged, are very suitable :—

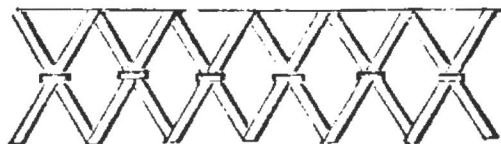

Various suggestions have been made for altering
the form of espalier trellises, but let the gardener
never adopt any that declines from the perpendicular.
The smallest approach to the horizontal increases the
radiation of heat from the trees, and increases, consequently, the cold they have to endure at night. It is
not one of the least advantages of training gooseberries
and currants as espaliers, that it facilitates the protecting them with mats.

Although on the borders the bushes are best trained

to stakes arranged lozenge-wise as above, yet in separate plantations they are preferably trained round hoops in this form.

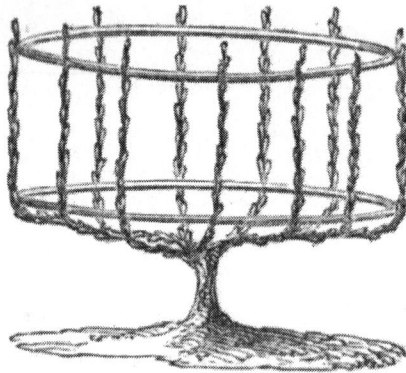

*Wall-training.*—Upon this branch of gooseberry culture, I have no better information to offer than is contained in the following very correct observations of Mr. Levingston, premising, however, that when so grown the fruit is forwarder, handsomer, and better flavoured than if grown upon standards.

Gooseberries do well trained against walls and palings ; the proper kinds for this purpose being the largest and most early sorts, such as the (Red) Crown-bob, Huntsman, Top-sawyer ; (Yellow) Nelson's-waves, Viper, Rockwood ; (Green), Ocean, Laurel, Independent ; (White), Smiling-beauty, Wellington's-glory, and Eagle. Plant them about six feet apart, in an open situation, where they can have the full benefit of the sun and air ; but if there is not a low wall in a good situation about the premises, they may be introduced into vacant spaces at the under parts of the wall, such as between rider trees.

Train them to the wall, &c., in a fan shape; keep
them regularly pruned and dressed to the wall; and
in every winter's pruning, observe to cut out all old
wood, and retain as much of the young as is necessary, laying in the young shoots at full length, and at
regular distances from each other. Look over them
at different times during the spring and summer, and
remove a great portion of the over-abundant young
wood, and nail in the remainder, that they may not
shade the advancing fruit. Give them gentle waterings in hot weather during the summer, until within
about a fortnight of the fruit being ripe; after which
the less moisture they have the better will be the flavour of the fruit. (*Levingston's Growth of the Gooseberry*, 40.)

*Root-pruning.* When planted the roots should be
without a tap root, and all spreading in a single whorl
from the base of the stem. They will always do so
if the cutting from which the shrub was raised was
not planted with more than three inches of its length
below the surface of the soil.

Of the established bushes, Mr. Saul, already noticed, says—

The roots should be pruned every two or three
years. When a root, therefore, has extended too far
from the stem, let it be uncovered, and all the strongest leaders shortened back nearly one half of their
length, and covered in with fresh marly loam. This

will cause new and more active roots to be formed
nearer the stem, and give the whole tree new vigour.
(*Gard. Mag.* iii. 422.)

There is a continual tendency on the part of the
under-ground buds to become branches, and these are
the suckers that we find so troublesome in many
kinds of soils.   By continually stopping and wounding them, however, they will, in general, perish ; and
to do this is what we recommend.   The Lancashire
gooseberry growers adopt the following as the best
means of preventing gooseberries from throwing up
suckers, and also an excellent plan of insuring an
abundance of large fruit.   In the sketch, A is the
bush, B B is the soil taken out about eighteen inches
all round the plant, and about six inches deep at C,

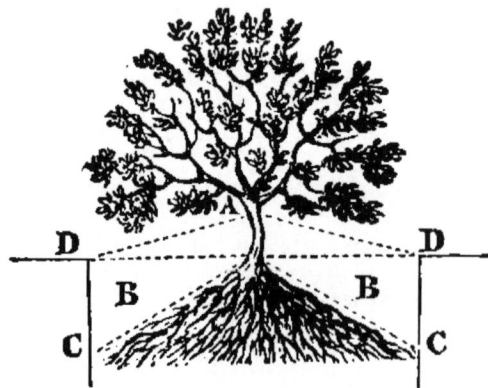

that if there are any buds or suckers, they are sure
to be seen and destroyed.   This do every year in
December, and as soon as the soil is taken out, spread
cowdung over the roots as shown at B, after which
replace the earth that has been taken out.   When you
have any new seedlings to propagate, do not take out

the soil, but lay the manure round them, and cover it with a layer of earth which encourages the plant to produce suckers. Raising from suckers, however, is not a mode of propagation of which I approve.

*Fruit.*—This should be thinned, the smaller berries being cut away with a pair of scissors for tarts, &c. as required, and the fine berries left for dessert. If some of reds, as the Warrington, and of the thick skinned yellows, as the Mogul, are matted over when the fruit is ripe, they will remain good until Christmas. This is easiest done when the tree is grown as an espalier.

*Large Fruit.* In Lancashire, where premiums are given for large gooseberries, without consideration of their table excellencies, the growers suffer only two or three to remain on each branch, and then, by supporting a saucer under each of these, bathe them for some weeks in so much water as to cover about a fourth part of each berry, which they call appropriately, though not elegantly, "*suckling the gooseberry.*"

Great attention and judgment are required to attain the effect desired from this practice, for if kept in the water too long, and at a time when ripeness is far advanced, the berries are liable to burst, or "to coddle," which is an ulceration arising from excessive moisture. To prevent the access of too much moisture to gooseberries ripening and intended for exhibition,

M

the growers shelter them as assiduously as the florist shades his flowers, and this is absolutely necessary, for when nearly ripe a very slight wetting of the berry's skin causes its bursting.

*Autumn Dressing.*—At the time of this season's pruning it is highly beneficial to brush the stems, and syringe the bushes with a strong brine of common salt. This destroys moss and the larvæ of insects, as well as gives a salutary stimulus to the bark.

Mr. J. Naismith, gardener at Culloden House, adopted a somewhat similar treatment, though with a less simple liquid. He says—

As soon as the leaves are all fallen, begin pruning and dunging, if necessary, then dig the ground between the bushes, leaving the ground as rough as possible; and as the diggers proceed, that is, as soon as they are clear of the first plant in the row, give the bush, from the rose of a water-pot, at least an English gallon of a mixture, in equal parts, of lime-water, chamber-ley, and soap-suds, in which is mixed as much soot as gives the composition the colour and consistence of rich dunghill drainings; proceeding over the whole in this manner, without treading or poaching the ground. When the winter frosts are fairly past, level and dress the ground between the shrubs with the rake. (*Cal. Hort. Soc. Mem.* ii. 90.)

The following is another application, of use in protecting the buds of gooseberries from the ravages of birds in the winter and spring months, as well as like the last, being effectual for clearing the bark of fruit-trees, generally, from moss, lichens, and the larvæ of insects. Take unslacked lime and soot, in equal quantities, add cow's urine until the mixture has attained the consistency of thick paint. Paint the trees regularly over with the mixture, and the result will be not only a clean bark, but an increased vigour in those trees to which the mixture has been so applied. (*Gard. Chron.* 1841. 85.)

---

## FORCING.

Neither the gooseberry nor currant can be forced without great care. No heat must be applied when they are first put under glass. A very low temperature, about 60 deg. and not higher than 40 deg. at night, must be employed afterwards, otherwise an excess of leaves and weak shoots are produced, but no fruit. When the fruit is well grown the temperature may be increased about 10 deg. For this purpose the plants to be forced are best grown in pots, small three year olds being selected, and placed in them at the end of October. In January move them into the peach house, and by careful treatment fruit will be ripe upon them in the course of April. The bush and its fruit may be sent to table.

Rifleman, Rumbullion, and Wilmot's Early are the best varieties for forcing.

To bring the fruit forward for tarts, the Rumbullion may be grown against a south wall, and sheltered with a glass case of the following form. The berries will be fit for the desired purpose in the course of March.

With a hinge at each of the upper corners, the light may be opened whenever air is desired to be admitted; the angle at which the glass is placed allows the inlet of more rays of light than if it were perpendicular; and being in form very like a common garden-frame, it may be so employed at all other seasons of the year.

This shelter need not be put over the shrub until the first week of January. In fine mild weather, the shrub may be sprinkled with tepid water, and the glass opened to admit air, but kept carefully closed at night, and during frosty weather.

## DISEASES.

*Blistering of the leaf* occurs occasionally, but not so frequently as to the currant. It arises from the parenchyma of the leaf swelling to a size not containable between the surrounding nerves or ribs of the leaf, and appears to be caused by the roots supplying more sap than the leaves can elaborate, and the blister rises in the effort made to increase the surface of leaf. The blister becomes red because an acid is formed by fermentation from the juices of the leaf mixing, owing to their rupture of the containing vessels. The disease is so circumscribed in its occurrence, and attacks so few leaves, that it is of little consequence, and does not require the adoption of any remedial treatment. If the blisters were ever to appear excessively, they would probably disappear by pruning in the roots as recommended in a previous section, and by well draining the soil. This is an effective remedy for a very similar disease affecting the peach leaf.

*Coddling* is an ulceration of the berry. It arises from excessive wet, for it is never found on a well drained soil, nor in very dry seasons. Sometimes the skin of the berry bursts, but as often the rupture is confined to its interior vessels, in consequence of which the mucilaginous and saccharine juices mingle, and decomposition ensues. The progress of this is apparent from the white coddled discoloration visible through the skin, on the side where the disease is progressing. At first the sugar of the berry decreases and a little alcohol is developed, imparting to it a vinous flavour, but this is rapidly followed by acetous fermentation, and eventually mouldiness and putrefaction destroy it. Good drainage of the soil, and sheltering the bushes from excessive rain, are the preventions of the disease. There is no cure for it when it does appear.

## INSECTS.

MANY are the insect marauders of the gooseberry, but the following are those of which we are chiefly cognizant :

*Aphis ribis* is a species of louse, preying both on the gooseberry and red currant. Its colour is blackish; and, like all other aphides, is injurious by its multitude; for although each consumes but a minute quantity of a plant's sap, yet, when thousands unite in their attacks, they very seriously injure its growth and prevent its developments. Even when fewer in number their excrements clog the pores of the leaves, and render the fruit disgusting. The most effectual mode of destroying them is to cover the infected bush with a sheet or other large envelope that will reach to the surface of the soil on all sides, and then to fumigate it with tobacco smoke.

The following are the best modes of fumigating; the first mode being the speediest, and the second the cheapest.

One or more pieces of cast iron, one inch thick, and three inches over, are to be made red hot (pieces of old tiles, such as are used for covering smoke flues, would probably answer equally well); and one of these being placed in a twenty-four sized pot, put on it the fourth of an ounce, or other quantity, of tobacco considered necessary to charge the space within the envelope with smoke sufficient to destroy insect life. This mode has these advantages—the tobacco is so quickly consumed, that the envelope is completely filled in a very short time, and but little smoke can escape before the insects are destroyed, the pure heat from the heater prevents injury from gas, and as no blowing is required there is no dust.

Another very simple mode of fumigating is as follows:—Dissolve a table-spoonful of saltpetre in a pint of water; take pieces of the coarsest brown paper, six inches wide, and ten inches long, steep them thoroughly in the solution, dry them and keep till wanted. To fumigate, roll one of the pieces into a pipe like a cigar, leaving the hollow half an inch in diameter, which fill with tobacco; twist one end and stick it into the soil; light the other, and it will burn gradually away for an hour or more.

Tobacco smoke should not be admitted to fruit trees when in bloom, nor when the fruit is ripening, as it imparts to them a flavour. (*Johnson's Dict. Mod. Gard.*)

*Tenthredo Grossulariæ.*—Mr. Curtis says, that this saw-fly was described, in 1823, by a French author, Le Pelletier de Saint Fargeau, under the name of *Nematus Trimaculatus;* and it is also called *N. Ribesii.*

The fly is of an ochreous colour; the antennæ are almost as long as the body, setaceous, brown above, and nine-jointed, the two basal joints being small; the crown of the head, the eyes, three large united spots on the centre of the trunk, as well as a large patch on the breast or sternum, are black; the body is orange, sometimes bright; the wings, which expand two-thirds of an inch, are iridescent; the reticulated nervures, the thickened costal edge of the superior wings, terminated by a callus spot, called the stigma, are brown; as are also the tips of the hinder-shanks, and their tarsi, or feet. The flies emerge, unheeded, from their tombs the beginning of April, and the female soon deposits her eggs close to the sides of the principal nervures on the underside of the leaves, which is very remarkable, for all the females of this extensive family are furnished with an instrument called the saw, for the purpose of cutting into the leaves and stalks, and introducing the eggs between the cuticles, or under the bark.

In about a week, the larvæ hatch, and commence feeding on the leaf on which they are stationed, and soon riddle them full of small holes; thus they go on feeding and changing their successive skins as they increase in size, until they are three-fourths of an inch long, when they are seen scattered round the edges of a partly-demolished leaf, holding by their fore legs, with their tails turned up, or lying on one side. At this time they are dull pale green; the first thoracic segment is deep yellow, and the penultimate of the same colour; the head, feet, and tail, are black, and each segment is dotted with the same colour, some of them having twenty-four spots, ranged in rows, down the back, those on the sides being more irregular, and one near the base of each foot is large; every one of these black tubercles produces a hair; they have six pectoral, sharp, horny feet, with which they always hold fast; the fourth segment seems to be destitute of feet, but the six following are each furnished with a pair of fleshy legs, which assist them in walking, and there is a similar part at the extremity of the last segment. There seems to be a succession of broods, from the early spring until October, occasionally; but the greatest numbers are congregated in May, and in the beginning of June.

Having defoliated a bush, leaving nothing of the leaves, excepting the footstalks, and sometimes a portion of the main rib, and being arrived at maturity, they cast their skins again, and then lose all their black spots, becoming of a uniform pale green, with two little black dots on the head, the spaces behind it and towards the tail retaining the yellow tint.

After resting awhile, they descend into the earth, and spin a yellow-brown cocoon, formed of silk and gluten, of so thick a texture that it is impervious; from these the summer broods of flies come up in less than three weeks, but the autumnal ones remain in them, curled up in the larvæ state, until the following spring, when they change to pupæ in time to produce flies, as the currant and gooseberry trees are coming into leaf. There are two modes of proceeding to rid our gardens of this terrible scourge; to catch flies, or search for the eggs and cut off the infested leaves, is scarcely practicable : our plan is, therefore, to look for the caterpillars; for, small as they are at first, they are easily detected by the perforated leaves, and when half-grown they are visible enough, and after that period they commit the greatest havoc, having inordinate appetites, and scarcely ceasing from their gluttony, except when their jackets become so tight that they are obliged to change. Hand-picking is, therefore, attended with great success in small gardens, but in plantations it is easier to sprinkle strong lime-water, as it is termed, over the leaves.

which will destroy the caterpillar; or syringe the bushes well, and then dust them with quicklime, having previously laid a good quantity round the stem, to prevent their re-ascending the bush : it is said, also, that water, heated to 140 degrees Fahren., and thrown forcibly upon the bushes, through the rose of an engine or watering-pot, will kill the larvæ, without injuring the tenderest leaves on the bushes. The other method alluded to is, to destroy the pupæ; and this seems to be best effected by scraping away the earth from the roots early in the spring, and drawing it into a deep trench between the bushes, covering it over, and trampling it well down. If boiling hot water be used, either in autumn or spring, to kill the pupæ, it should be put on the earth when it is quite dry ; the soil must be lifted two inches, and returned as soon as the water is poured in, that, as the heat passes off, it may destroy the animals encased in their shells. (*Gard. Chron.* 1841. 548.)

*White Caterpillars,* otherwise called *Borers,* are not so numerous as the other kinds, though very destructive. They bore the berry, and cause it to drop off. They preserve themselves during the winter season in the chrysalis state, about an inch under ground, and become flies nearly at the same time with the last-mentioned kind. They lay their eggs on the blossoms, and these eggs produce young caterpillars in May, which feed on the berries till they are full-grown, and they creep down into the earth, where they remain for the winter in the pupa state. (*Caled. Hort. Soc. Memoirs*, i. 102.)

*Phalæna (Abraxas) Grossulariata.* Mr. Curtis observes that this is one of our most striking and beautiful "Geometræ," and commonly known as the "Magpie" moth. There are few gardens where it may not be seen flying in the evening, towards the end of July, or resting with its wings closed under a leaf or against the side of a wall during the day. After pairing, the females lay their eggs upon a leaf, from which the little looping caterpillars hatch in September; and, living through the winter, they begin to feed again in the spring, and are not full-grown until the third week in May, and sometimes it is the end of June before they become pupæ; in about three weeks from that time the moths appear, and are consequently found from the middle of June to the end of July, or later, according to the temperature of the season. When these larvæ abound, which they mostly do on bushes, under old walls or hedges, they frequently strip the red currant and gooseberry bushes of their leaves, nothing but the footstalks being left. They will sometimes attack the sloe, and even the peach and almond tree. It is a handsome caterpillar when full-grown, forming a graceful loop as it walks, from which circumstance

such insects have been called Geometræ : it is slightly
hairy, of a cream colour, spotted with black, having
orange spots down the sides, so that it greatly resembles the moth in colour, which is very unusual.
Having arrived at maturity, it spins a web, so loosely
constructed that sometimes the pupa falls out; it is
either attached to the twigs, or concealed in crevices
in walls, palings, &c. The chrysalis is shining black,
with a few orange rings round the segments of the
body. The moth is of a cream colour, the spots
black ; the thorax and abdomen, a space near the
base of the upper wings, as well as an oblique stripe
beyond the centre, are of a fine orange colour; the
horns are a little the thickest in the males, but not
pectinated, as is often the case in this family. (*Gard.
Chron.* 1841, 515.)

*Phalæna Vanaria* is smaller than the preceding,
and, like it, abundant in our gardens during June and
July. The horns of the male are pectinated ; the
wings are of an ash colour, and freckled ; the upper
have four brown marks on the superior margin ; the
second crossing the centre of the wing, and forming
a V or L. The larva is a looper, having only ten
legs ; it infests the red currant and gooseberry bushes,
feeding upon the leaves, and is found in May. It is
about an inch long, bluish green, with two white
dorsal and two yellow lateral lines ; it is dotted with
little black tubercles, which produce short black hairs ;

it changes late in May to a chesnut-coloured chrysalis in a slight web, on the surface of the earth. As the young caterpillars are brought to life almost as soon as the leaves unfold, they are often as injurious as those of the magpie-moth. They may also be collected by hand-picking; but as they undergo their metamorphoses upon the earth, lime and hot water may be employed. (*Ibid.* 516.)

For the destruction of the caterpillars, fumigation with tobacco, as detailed for that of the aphis, may be effectually adopted, besides which the following modes have been suggested.

Mr. James Jackson says, in the month of February or March put under each gooseberry bush a piece of unslacked lime about the size of a turnip, pour water on it, and as soon as the lime separates mix it regularly with the earth under the bush so low as the roots. More is not necessary, nor will it be requisite (in general cases) to repeat the lime for three or four years. The fact is, the butterfly deposits its eggs during the summer under the bushes, which eggs the lime destroys. The lime should invariably be used before the leaves begin to make their appearance. (*Gard. Chron.* 1841, 366.)

Lime applied as above may prevent the moth depositing its eggs, or may destroy these and the pupæ within the soil, but it cannot prevent the moth laying her eggs upon the leaves. To destroy the caterpillars when hatched, white hellebore (*Veratrum album*) is most effectual, and may be employed in the following modes.

Mr. Groom, florist, Walworth, says, make a strong decoction of the root of the white hellebore, with some green tops of the elder; one pound of the hellebore-root and a good handful of elder-tops to one gallon of water. By syringing the trees with the liquid when cold, it will kill the caterpillars. Mr. Groom says the day should be fine, that the liquid may be dried on the leaves, as the caterpillars are destroyed by eating the leaves on which the poison has dried.

This theory seems erroneous, inasmuch as from the following statement made by Mr. Lymburn, it appears that the mere contact of the powder of the hellebore with the skin of the caterpillar causes its death.

The way to use it, is while one of the men holds up the branches and exposes the under side of the leaves, to dust the caterpillars with powder from the finger and thumb, wherever the caterpillars are to be seen; if the powder is dry, and if not it should be toasted before the fire, it is dispersed into a cloud, and wherever a particle reaches the caterpillars, they may be seen to collapse as if stabbed, and in an hour or two nothing but the skin is left. Some prefer dusting up from below with a puff, without examining where the caterpillars are, by which there is more waste of powder and less trouble. *(Gard. Chron.* 1841, 533*).*

Mr. J. Mackray, gardener at Errol House, gives the following as an effectual receipt: boil ¼lb. of tobacco with 1lb. of soft soap in about 18 Scots pints of water, and keep stirring the liquid while boiling with a whisk in order to dissolve the soap; this liquor when milk-warm, or so cool as not to hurt the foliage, apply to the bushes with a hand-squirt in the evening. The soap adheres to the leaves longer and closer than tobacco juice alone would do. *(Cal. Hort. Soc. Mem.* i. 272).

Mr. S. Elliot, gardener to Sir T. G. Carmichael, recommends the following compound for the same purpose: six pounds of black currant-leaves and as many of elder-leaves, boiled together in twelve gallons of soft water; put fourteen pounds of unslacked lime into twelve gallons of water, mix the two liquids together, and wash with the mixture the infested bushes and trees by means of the hand engine; after that is done, take a little hot lime and lay it at the root of each bush or tree that has been washed; which completes the operation. The caterpillars are thus destroyed without hurting the foliage of the bush. A dull day is to be preferred to any other for washing. When the foliage is all off the bushes and trees, wash them over with the hand engine to clear them of decayed leaves; for this purpose any sort of water will do. Then stir up the surface of the earth all round the roots to destroy the eggs. The above mentioned proportion of leaves, lime and water, will serve for two acres of ground or more, covered with bushes in the ordinary manner, and will cost very little. *(Cal. Hort. Soc. Mem.* i. 266).

## USES.

THE gooseberry is chiefly cultivated as a dessert fruit, and for that purpose some of its varieties are most' excellent. When grown with a sole attention to the increase of the size of the berry, this is very frequently rendered a mass of insipidity, but great increase of size and extreme lusciousness of flavour are not at all incompatible, for I have tasted the Pitmaston Greengage Gooseberry and the White Eagle, grown against a wall, the first weighing more than 12 dwts., and the second over 20 dwts., yet rivaling in flavour and lusciousness many fruits of much higher pretensions.

The gooseberry is also used in the preparation of many kinds of confectionery, both when unripe and ripe, and in the former state it is preserved in bottles for winter use in tarts. It is also employed for the manufacture of vinegar, spirit, and wine. On this last use, as being most nearly connected with the cultivator's art, I will append the following observations from the pen of Dr Macculloch.

The gooseberry is one of the fruits most commonly used, and is in particular well known as an ingredient in brisk wines, which are made to resemble, in appearance at least, the wines of Champagne. For this purpose it is used in an unripe state. It is well known in the wine countries that, independently of some other causes of briskness, this property always results ftom the use of unripe fruit, and is readily produced by mixing unripe grapes with the ripe ones. The case is the same with the gooseberry. The fault of this wine, however, if it be considered as an imitation of Champagne, is a bad flavour, which is almost invariably communicated by the fruit, and that in proportion to its ripeness. To avoid this evil, so generally injurious to the brisk gooseberry wines, the fruit can scarcely be taken in a state too crude, as at this period the flavouring substance has not been developed. At the same time, the expressive juice alone should be used, care being taken to exclude the skins from the fermentation, as being the part in which the flavour principally resides. With these precautions, the noxious flavour may generally be prevented. It is true, that the produce is then without flavour, or nearly so, but this is by much the most tolerable fault in domestic wines, whose leading defect is almost invariably a disagreeable taste. Various proportions of fruit and sugar are used by different persons; but the most common consist of 3lbs. of sugar and 4lbs. of fruit, to 8lbs. of water. Here the proportion of fruit is too small compared to that of the sugar, and the fermentation is consequently, in general, so imperfect as to leave the wine disagreeably sweet. At the same time, the proportion of sugar is such as to render the wine stronger than the strongest wines of Champagne. If, therefore, this wine is to be amended in composition, it is either by reducing the sugar, if we are contented with a weaker wine, or by increasing the fruit, if we are desirous of retaining the greater strength. In managing the fermentation to a constant and successful result, the rules laid down as practised for Champagne wine are strictly applicable in the present case; and with these precautions and practices carefully attended to, the produce of the gooseberry will be invariably successful. I may also add, that it is perfectly durable, as much so as Champagne wines of corresponding quality, provided equal care be taken in the bottling, the cellarage, and other management; all of them circumstances in which our domestic fabricators are too apt to fail, thinking that when they have mixed together a portion of sugar and fruit their labour is finished, and that the rest may be trusted to chance. They should consider, on the contrary, that it is but then commenced. From the gooseberry in a ripe state wines may be also made, for which no rules are required. But the produce of the ripe fruit is commonly ill-flavoured, and, whether sweet or dry, is scarcely to be rendered palateable, unless, perhaps, by a most careful exclusion of the husks. (*Cal. Hort. Soc. Mem.* ii. 187.)

WINCHESTER:
PRINTED BY H. WOOLDRIDGE, HIGH-STREET.

Printed in Great Britain
by Amazon